POORLY WRAPPED GIFTS

RISING AND THRIVING AFTER INFIDELITY

Sujata Patel

http://poorlywrappedgifts.com

Copyright Page

Poorly Wrapped Gifts © Copyright 2023 by Sujata Patel

Published in the United States by A Happy New World Publishing, an imprint of Wellness with Sujata, LTD, Ohio.

Although the author and publisher have made every effort to ensure that the information in this book was correct at press time, the author and publisher do not assume and hereby disclaim any liability to any party for any loss, damage, or disruption caused by errors or omissions, whether such errors or omissions result from negligence, accident, or any other cause.

Adherence to all applicable laws and regulations, including international, federal, state, and local governing professional licensing, business practices, advertising, and all other aspects of doing business in the US, Canada or any other jurisdiction is the sole responsibility of the reader and consumer.

Neither the author nor the publisher assumes any responsibility or liability whatsoever on behalf of the consumer or reader of this material. Any perceived slight of any individual or organization is purely unintentional.

The resources in this book are provided for informational purposes only and should not be used to replace the specialized training and professional judgment of a health care or mental health care professional.

Neither the author nor the publisher can be held responsible for the use of the information provided within this book. Please always consult a trained professional before making any decision regarding treatment of yourself or others.

For more information, email info@journeywithsujata.com.
ISBN: 979-8-89109-232-7 - paperback
ISBN: 979-8-89109-233-4 - ebook

For every woman rising and finding her way

ACKNOWLEDGMENTS

I HAVE IMMENSE GRATITUDE FOR ALL the people who helped make this book a reality.

Thanks to everyone on my publishing team. Thanks to Kerk, my writing coach, who held me accountable and encouraged me along the way. To my editor, Thea, who helped shape this book, providing me with valuable insight as we took my first draft and made it into something readable.

To Liz, who has been there every step of the way in EVERY way, encouraging me to write, talking things through, helping me process unhealed wounds, and celebrating my wins.

To Susanne for supporting me in my desire to write this book over seven years ago and for her insight and infusions of courage over the years.

To my friends and family who haven't judged me for writing about such a sensitive topic. I thank you for remaining open and understanding why I had to write this book.

To my parents, who came to the United States over sixty years ago. Had they not come, I would not have had the luxury of using my voice to write about such an intimate topic. To my mom for her amazing courage in life to take giant leaps, with an uncertain future, inspiring me to do the same. To my dad, who prioritized education and free thinking and has paved the way for me to have the time to write about what lights me up so that I can make a difference.

Deep, profound, heartfelt gratitude for Nick for his loving support of me writing this book. For encouraging me to use my voice to tell my story and stand in my power. His support has given me the courage and peace I needed to complete this project. I couldn't have done it without him. Despite the vulnerable topic, he stands in his sacred space and loves me for standing in mine. I thank him for his hard work and his commitment to us, and his desire to always work to be a better version of himself. And for his encouragement of me to do the same. I thank him for showing up every single day. For those of you who have loved him, I thank you for continuing to do so. Hurt people hurt people, and it is with constant awareness, immense compassion, merciful grace, repeated forgiveness, and deep love that all can be healed.

And finally, thank you to my children, for being the inspiration for everything I do.

CONTENTS

INTRODUCTION

LEARNING THAT YOUR SIGNIFICANT OTHER has been having an affair can be one of the most devastating moments of your life. It feels like a sucker punch to the gut. The rug has been swept out from under you. Your head spins. You don't know up from down. Everything feels out of control. You fall to the ground, wondering if you will ever be able to breathe again and lift yourself up.

I have never been in a romantic relationship where the man did not cheat on me. We didn't have an open relationship, and it was explicitly agreed that our relationship was one that would be monogamous.

My first marriage ended because of infidelity. I didn't really suffer from a broken heart—it was fear of not having my kids full time. It was the end of how I imagined life was supposed to be. I felt like I was losing my personal power. I didn't make the decision to leave because my husband made it for me. And when he did, a big weight lifted off me.

Days after finding out about my ex-husband's affair, I purchased a dozen books on how to handle the affair and on forgiveness...all the classics such as *After the Affair*, *The Dance of Anger*, and *How to Heal your Relationship*. (It was great—it only required the participation of one member of the relationship). I even subscribed to a few online healing programs and printed out the manuals with great intentions to go through them with my husband.

Back then, we went to a counselor together, ONCE. When the counselor discovered that the reason my husband was no longer with his mistress (because I scared her off), she called me a vindictive bitch. Right there. In her "safe space" of an office. WOW.

What I gathered from that counselor was that there was a proper way to respond when you find out your husband is having an affair and when you feel like your whole family unit is crumbling. Apparently, the loving thing to do when in the shock and anger stages of grief of your marriage ending is to support the loving couple who is breaking up your life. This counselor reinforced every bit of archaic "wisdom" of how a woman should behave when her man transgresses. Clearly, this was a counselor who had her own set of issues and was in no way capable of offering usable guidance. I never went back.

I sarcastically referred to the unveiling of my husband's affair as "the big reveal." Often the phrase "big reveal" has connotations of something positive and grand. When watching a home makeover show, the big reveal shows us the marvelous transformations made to a house. Or when Oprah used to give out surprise gifts to her audience. You're just sitting there living your life, taking in a show, and *SURPRISE!*

With a big reveal, everything changes. It happens in an instant. While my big reveal was neither marvelous nor fun, I have grown to view the big reveal as a gift. It just didn't come wrapped in a pretty package. I lovingly refer to experiences like this as my "poorly wrapped gifts."

You can imagine how disappointed I was when the big reveal happened in my current relationship. *Why in the hell did I throw out all of those books I paid good money for when my ex-husband cheated on me?*

Because I didn't ever think I would be in this position again.

It was different this time around, though. This affair hit me harder than the one with my ex-husband. I had more of my heart invested this time around. I felt my heart break into a million pieces. The triggers hit me harder. The self-doubt hit me harder. Blindsided, I had new gaping wounds, which opened old wounds and lit up all of my insecurities.

How could I have missed this? What the hell was wrong with me? And why in the hell was I not running for my life? Was I THAT pathetic that I would actually consider working it out with this man and seeing where we end up?

I was scared. I felt abandoned and rejected.

I was devastated. I felt powerless and out of control. I felt crazy at times, and embarrassed that I had chosen to stay with him. I had one foot in and one foot out, ready to run but also frozen. I felt like my triggers were drowning me, and I didn't know how to handle them.

I didn't know what to do. I didn't know where to start.

When I started trying to process my intense feelings and emotions after learning about the affair, I felt very alone. There were no easily accessible resources that normalized the ups and downs I was navigating. Friends couldn't handle the intensity of what brewed inside of me. Counselors sat silently as I regurgitated my story over and over. The books I found felt clinical and sterile, and I couldn't find anything that validated my experience. And I needed help with my triggers. They were pounding my nervous system nonstop, and I didn't have the skills to cope with them yet.

I started writing this book in 2018. Over the years, each time I wrote, it took me right back to being triggered and being angry as hell. It felt like I was taking several steps backward when I wanted to move forward and feel better. For that reason and for many others, I stopped writing this book several times.

I also wanted to protect my personal life and my man. Not everyone knew about what we were going through, and I didn't want either of us to lose the respect of friends and family over me writing a book that put our lives on display.

But over the months and years, the Universe kept whispering to me: *Write the book.*

One day in meditation, clarity came to me. The ideas for this book popped into my head. Importantly, I had clarity about WHY I wanted to write the book and who I wanted to talk to. It had to be relatable. I would tell my story like I would share it with a friend. It had to be the resource I could have used when I was going through the thick of my pain.

I wrote this for all the women and men who have felt alone on their journey. For those who have been told they are crazy or that they need to let it go and never speak of it again. For those who have been repeatedly told, "It's been___ years. Aren't you over this by now?" For those who are unconventional, who have real human emotions, who haven't been able to get the validation they seek for any part of the process. For those who have sought therapy only to be met with half-brained quacks who bring their own baggage into the counseling session. For those who have plenty of input from friends and family, urging them to think differently, feel differently, or go against what feels right for them. For those who lost confidence or hope. And I am also writing this book for those of you who are curious and just want to know what the hell happened in my home. It is all good.

I humbly share my experiences with as much candor and authenticity and vulnerability as I can muster. It is my hope that in reading this book you will take whatever lessons and tools resonate with you and gain the hope that you can make your life spectacular even after a life-changing event like an affair. I hope that through reading this book, you feel supported and not so alone. Like someone else also gets it. I want you to feel validated and in control of your healing. I want you to take charge of your growth, discover new things about yourself, and empower yourself.

If I can play even the smallest role in helping you navigate this tough road or making your life amazing, then my struggles, my pain and suffering, and me opening my life to the world, have been worth it. When I can turn a horrible event into something helpful, it transmutes energy and helps me heal at a deeper level. My experience then serves a purpose. And I need it to not have been in vain. I need it to mean something.

Some of life's most precious gifts come in poorly wrapped packages. This is my story of tearing through the ugly packaging and revealing the gifts contained within.

For those of you who have been on the receiving end of infidelity, I share my story to offer hope and let you know you are not alone. And not only will you survive this, but you can eventually find a way to thrive. You can feel joy again.

There is more than one way to get there. My path is one path. You will forge your own. I share some of the key choices and experiences that made a difference in my healing—what propelled me and what held me back. I share my experiences with counselors, my grief process, my biggest challenges, and my big-shift moments. I write about trust, forgiveness, intimacy, and moving forward. I share my growth and transformation process in the hope that you will find something in my story that resonates with you and moves you in the direction of growth and peace.

In parts two and three of this book, I list key points to re-member at the end of each chapter. After you read the book, feel free to keep it as a quick and easy resource.

At the end of the book, I have included an appendix with a self-care guide as well as a compilation of some major points to remember as you walk along your path. They are in no particular order but are some simple but powerful reminders based on what lessons I learned and messages I wish I had heard more often. I also provided links to some of the books I found useful as I journeyed through my healing.

I hope as you read this book, you get what you are looking for. I hope something stands out that speaks to you and makes a difference in your day, your week, your month, your life. My heart is with you as you journey forward on your path to healing.

PART 1

The Beginning

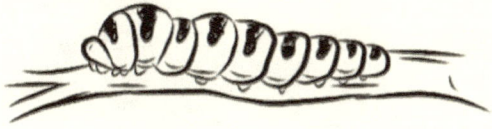

Caterpillar

CHAPTER 1

THE BIG REVEAL

I T WAS A GLORIOUS SPRING morning. We were up and ready to go by 7:00 a.m. The slight chill in the air gave it a comforting and invigorating smell. The sun was shining, and the skies were the perfect color of sky blue, like the Crayola Crayon color that used to be my absolute favorite. Nick and I were headed to the beach for spring break with seven kids in tow. Four of them were seniors in high school. He drove his SUV with two of his sons, a friend of his middle son, and my youngest son. I drove in a separate car with my oldest son and his girlfriend, along with my youngest daughter.

Nick arrived late at my house that morning and had texted that he was a bit peeved about being late. So, as he pulled into the driveway, I intentionally greeted him with extra love. I wrapped my arms around him, held him for a long time, and told him it was no big deal. We would get to our destination whenever we got there. It was the journey that mattered, not the destination. We would make it fun, despite our delayed start. We had no stress.

I felt so in love with him and was super excited to be heading on another family trip to the beach for a week of connecting, laughing, sharing, being silly, and relaxing. We had been on several family trips together over the years, and each one was magical. I knew this trip would be full of wonder too. Just days before, he had run up to me in my kitchen, wrapped his arms around me, and with the biggest smile, looked into my eyes and told me I was going to be his wife one day. My heart fluttered. We were both feeling it. We had been together for six years. And although we had considered marriage, we didn't want to blend our families during our children's late teenage years. We resolved to wait until they were in college because we didn't want to disrupt their lives. It worked well. He was close to my children, and I was close to his. We were basically a family living in two separate homes, which is why our family trips were extra special. We would all be under one roof, spending our days in the sun and water, staying up late laughing and pulling pranks. In the late evening, the kids would run off to do silly things and make their own memories together while Nick and I relaxed under the stars.

I love going on road trips with my kids and stopping at travel stations where we can all get gas station coffee—my favorite. We drove south, making a few stops along the way. We played music, and I sang my favorite songs in the car.

About eight hours into our trip, we stopped for lunch at the McDonald's at Exit 22 in Tennessee off Interstate 75. As with every other stop we made, I got out of the car with a huge smile and wrapped my loving arms around Nick. I held him close and breathed him in. He always smelled so good. I remember the innocence and deep love I felt for him in that extra-long hug. It was noteworthy.

It would be a long time before I would ever have that safe, secure, innocent, and deeply loving feeling again.

I went to the restroom and pulled out my phone to check my business emails. I had a relatively new business and was hoping to see new messages. Low and behold, I had eight emails. I wasn't sure if it was a spammer filling my inbox because I didn't recognize the sender's email address.

As it turns out, the emails were from a woman I knew. She was a coworker of Nick's. I was confused as I read the emails. They confessed to something that I couldn't grasp. She was showing me proof of an almost two-year affair with Nick, including screenshots of text messages and emails. I stood there in disbelief of what I was reading. As the adrenaline raced through my body, I couldn't fully comprehend the words I was reading, and I started to feel lightheaded.

I needed space. I left the confines of the restroom and stood near the ordering counter to try to read the first very lengthy email.

I remember standing there—the kids had ordered, and I had paid. The kids were all gathered in a large semi-circular booth a few steps away from me, waiting for their food. They were looking at me. I stood there reading and shaking. I could barely breathe.

Nick walked past me and saw who the emails were from and kept on walking, not saying a word.

As I gasped for air, I could barely get the words out that I needed to go outside and get some air. I was trembling. I could barely stand. My knees felt like they were buckling and were going to give out from underneath me. I could not breathe. My heart was pounding out of my chest. I felt lightheaded. I was dazed. I was in shock. *What?! This could not be true. No way in hell.*

I went back in and asked Nick if I could talk to him outside.

I sat down on the curb next to the car and asked him point blank, "Are you having an affair with Midge?" (I changed her name).

He simply replied, "Yes."

Nothing followed.

My head swirled from the shock. I got sick to my stomach and thought I was going to pass out. I didn't know what hit me. I didn't know what this meant. I was riddled with thoughts and questions. It just didn't make sense. *How could he?* Every thought came to me all at once. What the actual fuck was happening to my life right now?

I couldn't see straight. My whole life—everything I believed and felt about my security, my love, my everything—completely shattered in that instant.

I yelled "I hate you. I hate you. Fuck you. I hate you" over and over. I know I said more, but everything else that was said in that parking lot is a big blur. I was in shock.

Five minutes passed before we walked into McDonald's and told the kids it was time to go. As we walked back to the car, I walked ahead of the kids, trying to choke back my tears. I don't even know what my kids were thinking or looked like because I was so absorbed in trying to breathe and regain my composure. I was completely unaware that they had been watching me through the window as I yelled at Nick outside. I worked hard to get some full breaths of air into my lungs and into my brain. It was a strain at best.

As we were opening the doors to get inside the car, my oldest son asked me point blank why I was yelling at Nick. Well shit. I realized that at least one of the kids had been watching. I honestly do not know which other kids saw the interaction and were concerned. I was oblivious to everything that was going on around me as my world was spinning. But my precious son saw it. He saw the nonverbals and my lips moving in the general direction of "Fuck you, and I hate you." He witnessed the angry look on my face. That look of devastation, of disbelief. He saw the whole thing. He didn't know what in the world happened between that long drawn-out loving hug and now. What could have possibly happened in the last ten minutes to warrant this?

I am generally a peaceful person. I don't have huge mood swings. And I typically don't react emotionally. So, for my son to see this, it stood out. And he wanted answers. I told him I would tell him in the car.

I still had five more hours to drive in the car until we reached our destination for that night. I had to somehow keep my shit together. And all I really wanted to do was crawl up into a little ball and cry and scream and talk to Liz, my very best friend in the entire world, my rock, the other half of my brain. The one who has been there for every up and every down since my early twenties. My soul sister, who also happens to be married to my brother. But I didn't have the luxury of having a phone call with Liz because she was in an airplane traveling, and I had three kids in my car.

When we got in the car, my son asked again. I forced myself to take a deep breath to calm myself and told him I needed to get on the highway first.

Why would I tell my kids what happened? This felt like something I could not keep to myself if we were going to be in the car together. What if I had a breakdown and needed them to drive for me? I needed them to understand any potential emotional outbursts or tears that might start streaming down my face out of the blue. And I have always been up-front with them. Honestly, though, I don't think I went through this whole thought process to decide whether or not I would tell my kids. It was just something I did. He asked, I answered.

I prefaced my answer by telling his girlfriend, "I am so sorry in advance for what comes out of my mouth. I am going to try to keep it together and not cry. I am sorry you have to be here for this." Well, something to that effect…

And then I told them. I tried to hold it together. I tried to be safe on the road. I tried not to completely break. There was silence in the car. No one said a thing. Not one thing. I looked in the rearview mirror and saw their faces. They looked stunned, like they were in shock. Who wouldn't be? I have to imagine my son wished he hadn't asked. Or that I hadn't answered. Or that they could somehow teleport themselves out of that car to somewhere else. Anywhere. I am sure my son was hoping that his mother was being overreactive and unreasonable for something benign when I was yelling at Nick. That would be easy to grasp. My kids could have told me to be more patient and not yell at Nick. They could have stuck up for him. But this? There was no sticking up for him.

Just moments later as I was trying to gather myself from delivering this shocking news, my oldest daughter called me. She hadn't joined us on this trip because her college spring break didn't align with ours. When I saw her face on my caller ID, I knew someone had told her. I wasn't ready for this. I dreaded picking up the phone.

I took another deep breath and uttered a weak "Hi, honey," as I answered the phone. "How are you?"

She said her sister had texted her what appeared to be a very cruel April Fool's Day joke. Oh yes—did I happen to mention it was April 1? I let out a halfhearted chuckle and told her that sadly, it was not an April Fool's Day joke, and that I wished it was.

To which she responded, "Don't worry, Mom. We will get through this as a family."

My heart.

People have asked me why I didn't just turn around and drive straight home.

Why do we do anything when we have experienced something traumatic? I didn't make a conscious decision at that moment, but it seemed to be driven by doing what I needed to do for the kids. We had four high school seniors on the trip, and we were going to the beach. I didn't even entertain the thought of driving home. It didn't even cross my mind. I don't have another explanation as to why.

When we arrived at our stopping point for the night, Nick and his boys came to my family's suite. Nick had his tail between his legs and looked tired in the face and eyes. But he also reminded me of a little boy who had just gotten in trouble and was going to try to talk himself out of it. He briefly spoke to our roomful of kids about what he had done and apologized before he asked if he could talk to me. The kids all looked stunned and incredibly uncomfortable. Who wants to hear that their dad/mom's boyfriend had been having an affair?

I wanted to talk with him, but not in front of the kids. I should clarify—I wanted to unload my anger and rage on him. But first, I wanted to gather information. Oh, my information gathering skills! We went to his room while the kids hung out in mine. The conversation was chaotic. He had spent the last five hours of driving time figuring out how to spin this. He was certain that he could talk his way out of this and point the finger at me.

As we started talking, I began asking direct questions. Everything that came out of his mouth felt like a spin. He was talking in circles, so as not to provide too much incriminating evidence. As I asked questions, he threw the questions right back at me.

For example, when I asked if he had a problem with sex, he immediately fired back, "DO YOU?!"

I could not get a straight answer to save my life. Nothing that he was saying made sense. It felt like he was a small child using whatever manipulation skills he had to somehow distract me from the issue at hand. In my frustration, as I was sitting in a chair across from Nick, listening to his vague replies, I texted the mistress to ask her for facts. After all, in one of her emails, she told me to call her, and she would tell me everything. I asked very pointed questions, and she gave me very detailed answers—more than what I asked for—and everything I learned was devastating.

I still wish I could use a Brillo pad to scrub away the details that the text message exchange revealed. I could not wrap my head around all the things that were coming at me.

While Nick tried to deny facets of his affair, the mistress fired off questions for me to ask him, proving that he was lying. The questions started coming in faster than Nick could think to spin them.

I sobbed. Every time I turned around to catch my breath, another text came in. Then she went from being the "benevolent" affair partner to attacking me. She called me a "fat cow" and a "dumb Indian" and said that his karma would be living a miserable life with me. As if I didn't have enough information being thrown at me, I was also being verbally abused by someone who had already derailed my world that day. Classy. By now,

Nick and I were standing in the hotel hallway. The kids had gotten tired and wanted to go to sleep. As the text messages kept coming, as the name-calling continued, I threw my phone down the hallway. I could not take any more information.

We made our way into the stairwell to continue the argument. Nick's house of cards began to crumble. My nonstop firing off questions finally made it fall to the ground. He told me later that somewhere in there, he had a shift. I know he did. I was standing right in front of him, and I could see it on his face. I felt it in the shift of his energy. I heard it in all the words that followed, as he dropped all of his defensiveness and started talking. I heard it in his apologies, saw it in his tears as he cried. Later, I saw it as he spoke with his sisters on the phone, sobbing. I observed it in how he spoke with my children about it, and how he catered to my every need in the days, weeks, and years following the big reveal. Nick had been a very proud man. He had a big chip on his shoulder, and he would never be caught groveling. His former self would have just run the other way and been done with anything hard. He would certainly not take the kind of words I was throwing at him out of my intense hurt and anger.

When his house of cards fell, his face looked like a lightbulb came on. He sheepishly admitted that he had treated every woman in his life poorly. It was at this moment when he stopped pointing fingers at me and started pointing the fingers back at himself. His spinning of the entire situation stopped. He went from having his heels dug into the ground, defending himself and placing blame on me, to suddenly accepting full responsibility for his actions and showing care and concern about my world spinning out of control. It felt like this shift happened in the blink of an eye. It was unlike anything I had ever seen. I can't explain it. In his moment of realization, he became a river of straight answers. Whatever I asked him, he answered. And his tears of realizing who he had become started to flow.

In those moments, the heavy burden he had been carrying all of his life was magically lifted off him, and he would forever be on a new trajectory.

In those very same moments, all of my innocence, trust, and eternal optimism were crushed by the very same weight that had just been lifted off him. In those moments, my rosy world went dark. The weight of the sharp blow threw me to the ground and held me down. I could not catch my breath. And it would be a while before I would be able to.

I was a complete mess that night. In between my tears and my mind racing, I managed to get about ten minutes of sleep. And I still had to drive my kids four more hours to the beach. Oh. My. God!

We got in the car and drove. I played heartbreak music, and my sweet son took the phone and started playing all sorts of angry music—fuck this and fuck that, I hate you, etc. We rolled the windows down, blared the music, and sang at the top of our lungs. My son knew exactly what I needed. No words had to be exchanged. I wonder if he realizes how much his love, empathy, and understanding meant to me.

When we got to the condo, I walked down to the beach by myself. I was finally able to take a moment away from my kiddos, away from him. Just me and the vast ocean. Just me with myself and my thoughts. And my pain. Finally, some time to sit with my own emotions. I was still in shock. At first, I couldn't muster up tears that I needed to shed. I wanted to. But I just couldn't.

I begged the Universe to help me. I repeated, over and over, "HELP ME! HELP ME!" Finally, tears started streaming down my cheeks.

My stomach felt like there was a butcher's knife stuck in it and someone was twisting it with a smile on their face. "Help me! Help me!"

The betrayal cut through my core. This. Broke. My. Heart.

I gave myself about a half hour before I allowed my anger to seep back in and protect the frail parts of me that couldn't afford to crumble right now. I had to go back into survival mode to be whatever I needed to be for my kids. I slapped a smile on my face anytime I was around them. But they knew. They knew I was hurting. And so were they.

Nick came out to get me, and all I could do was cry. He was helpless. There was literally nothing he could do or say to fix this. We all sat down to eat, and as I looked around, I noticed Nick was not there. He had taken his bowl into the other room and sat down at a little table for two. I marched in there and told him this was not about him. That he would get his ass out there, sit at the table, put a damn smile on his face, and not make an already terrible situation more awkward for the kids. He did. And from that moment forward, he understood his role as far as the kids went.

When we were around the kids, I played it cool. All the focus was on them and on the wonder of being at the ocean, being together, being on spring break. But as soon as the doors closed, and I was faced with just Nick, a level of anger and rage that I had truly never known before seethed out of my mouth, my eyes, my ears, my sweat glands, my body. I did not care how it impacted him. As far as I was concerned, he deserved every bit of what he was getting from me.

I know we were all impacted by this betrayal. A betrayal like this doesn't just impact the couple. There is a whole ecosystem that is disrupted. In a big way. I wanted to do what I could to make it as manageable as possible for my kiddos.

I was lost. I felt empty. There was a void in me so large that I didn't know if I would ever be okay.

The first night at the beach was filled with tears and anger. It was terrible. Morning came—more tears. More conversation. I told him I didn't even know who the hell he was. I refused to do anything other than take care of myself that week.

I remember him carrying the beach chairs and umbrellas, the cooler, his hat, water bottles, and beach toys. And me standing just inside the door waiting for him to open the damn door for me. Every single time we went to the beach or returned back from the beach. This, in and of itself, was a version of Nick that I did not recognize. I expected him to do absolutely everything—cooking, cleaning, carrying the beach chairs and umbrellas. And he obliged. It was the least he could do.

He assumed all of these tasks without a single argument or negative facial expression. Even *I* thought some of my requests were a little unreasonable. But nevertheless, he quietly and co-operatively did whatever I asked.

Our first morning there, my first inclination was to stay in bed. I wanted so badly to do nothing but wallow in my great sadness. But I had just started training for a half marathon. And as much as I wanted to stop, fall to the ground, and hit eject, I vowed to keep going. I was not going to let him steal this from me. I was just recovering from being crippled in 2014 from an antibiotic, and this half marathon was my comeback. I needed this half marathon to prove to myself that I could do it. That I had indeed recovered from the most dreadful and debilitating experience I had endured in this life. I was not going to let a man get in the way of my goal. I used my anger and rage as fuel to go on my training run that morning and every other morning while we were there.

Throughout the week, there were many realizations that kept coming out as I continued to ask him questions. He kept answering truthfully, and with each revelation, I felt more and more devastated. My anger kept me from completely falling apart. It raged. It seethed. But it saved me.

In this world, and in many cultures, women are simply not allowed to be angry. We are looked down on as being hormonal, irrational, emotional, not put together and bitchy. In this same world, men have been allowed to express their barbaric anger for far less than their worlds falling apart.

Well, I didn't have that limiting belief. I knew that in order to heal, my anger had to come out. And who better to direct it to than the person or people who played a role in creating this experience for me?

Somewhere in the midst of all this rage and destruction, I had moments when I could connect to my thinking brain. I would walk the beach saying out loud to myself, "It's not what happens to you, but how you respond, that determines your physiological and emotional health." That was part of my meditation teacher certification class. It was a powerful message for me. I had used this line over and over with my clients. It is true, after all. It is how we respond to events and circumstances that determines our physiological and emotional health. I had no idea what lay ahead of me in the coming months. For the time being, though, I thought I had it all figured out. *I've got this.*

That week wasn't all bad. It was mixed in with laughter and making memories with the kids. Playing beach volleyball, watching my son and his girlfriend parasail, walking around the gigantic beach store over and over, playing hide and seek and laughing till I thought I was going to pee my pants, going to the all-you-can eat crab buffet, being with my girls who showed me so much love and compassion. I want to remember those good moments too. Because they matter. They are what got me through that week in one piece.

On the way home, we stopped at Exit 22 in Tennessee. My request.

When we entered the McDonald's parking lot, my daughter said, "Oh, it's THIS place."

I responded with, "No place keeps our power. We are here to reclaim it."

* * *

Well that completely and utterly sucked.

So how in the world did we end up there?

CHAPTER 2

I WISH I HAD A HUSBAND LIKE THAT

LET ME TAKE YOU BACK to the day our love story began. It was spring of 2009, and I was taking my eight-year-old son to soccer practice. He was on a new team with new coaches, and I was that overprotective mom who never left her kids with strangers. It was a beautiful, sunny day with a slight chill in the air. It smelled of springtime. I noticed mylar balloons tied to one of the coach's cars to let parents know that this was the place. A lot of the boys on the team were already there, and the coaches greeted the boys as they arrived. I walked my wonderful son over to the male coach and introduced myself, "Hi, my name is Sujata, and this is my son."

The coach replied, "Hi Sue," a common mistake people make. I corrected him. I might have even judged him a little for not being able to pronounce three syllables. But I get it. People think Sue is my first name and Jata is my last. I got so caught up with making sure he knew my name, I neglected to pay attention to what his name was. Also, a common occurrence.

I walked my other three kids to a playground within sight and earshot of soccer practice. As I pushed some of my kids on the swings, I watched the new coach with my son. He was encouraging and supportive. He was enthusiastic when he spoke, and he was very active with the team. I heard him say "Good job!" a lot, and then he would run around and show the young boys what to do next. He was super active on the field. He was also easy on the eyes. He was tan, had well-defined calves, and had a sweet smile. I approved of him being the coach for my precious son and a bit of eye candy for me as a soccer mom.

While I stood there watching him interact with and encourage the young boys, I heard a whisper in my head out of nowhere. "I wish I had a husband like that." It was clear as day. I remember it vividly because at the time it seemed weird because I thought my marriage was in a pretty good place. This wasn't a thought I would typically think or say out loud. I was living my life in suburbia, married with four amazing children. But this whisper came from a place deep within me. I would recognize years later that the Universe might have been telling me that something was awry in my marriage. But at the time I wasn't aware of WHY I heard those words. As quickly as I heard the whisper of those words, they faded into a memory. My kids and I left the swings and made our way to the monkey bars.

CHAPTER 3

MY MARRIAGE AT THE TIME

JEFF AND I HAD A good partnership. We owned a pharmacy, and we had a good division of labor between the two of us at work and home. We made it look easy. We were always on task. However, I remember times when I'd be talking to Jeff about something exciting that had happened during the day, only to be disappointed and deflated to see that he had fallen asleep in the chair. A few times, one of my children saw this interplay between us, and I just sighed and shook my head. It would take me a while to get the courage back up to share something exciting or something that brought me joy. I didn't want that joy to be squashed by a sleeping, less than enthusiastic husband. I remember thinking to myself, *what is going to happen to me when the kids grow up and are gone? Who will I talk to? And who will listen?*

It was around this time that I went for what felt like a memorable walk around the neighborhood. As I approached the road to my house, I said out loud to the Universe, *Okay. I will live out this lifetime with Jeff. He is not the love of all loves. And he is not my soulmate. But he gave me these four wonderful children, who I will do anything for. I will live this lifetime with Jeff, for my kids. I am more than okay with that. My children are my soulmates in this lifetime. And I know in my next lifetime, I will connect with the love of all of my lifetimes. The one who lights me up and makes my heart beat out of my chest. The one that touches my soul. I can wait. Thank you, Universe.*

By the summer of 2009, I had asked the Universe to give me an easy summer. No drama, no earth-shattering events. Just joyful, playful time with my four children. I had just completed the Big Sur marathon, my second marathon in a year, and I was excited for some downtime to just play. No marathon training schedule, no strict eating guidelines. (If you have trained for a marathon, you know that is another full-time endeavor.) That summer was the best. We went hiking at parks, swam in our pool, hosted get-togethers with friends and family. We traveled to Washington, DC, and then to a family reunion on Jeff's side of the family for Labor Day weekend.

During our trip to Washington, DC, I felt like something weird was happening. Jeff was always on his phone. And he spent an incredible amount of time in the bathroom. One time his phone buzzed, and I got up to hand it to him. He jumped up so fast to take the phone from me that I found it odd. In addition to that, one of the women from work sent me a message to see if it would be okay if they took Jeff out for his birthday. She wanted to check with me because she knew I would have to be home with the kids and wanted to be sure I was cool with that. This felt weird too because we all worked together. If there was going to be a work get-together, I should be included. I started thinking of several instances where things didn't feel right and made a note to myself to go home and check phone records. But by the time we got home, it slipped my mind. I was busy with my four kids. Their cousins spent a lot of time at our house, so at any given time, I had about seven to eight kids at my house. And I was still doing all the administrative work for our pharmacy business and running the household. No wonder it slipped my mind.

That summer, we had a family wedding to go to—on Jeff's side of the family. His estranged biological father, who he hadn't seen in nearly thirty years, was going to be in attendance. I knew this was a huge strain for Jeff. He hadn't quite worked through all the issues surrounding his father leaving when he was a young boy of seven. He told me he was going to take up running. And meditating. To help him handle whatever was coming up for him. Well, he said the magic words to me. Running. Meditating. Both things that I did that did wonders for my psyche. And that I had wanted to do with my husband.

He had all the freedom in the world to connect with running and meditating. Most nights, he worked at the pharmacy well into the evening and then went to the local Metro Park to run. He told me he was running three times around a loop we used to do. That was 9.3 miles total. I was impressed that he could do that kind of mileage right off the bat. I felt like an amateur. I had to slowly make my way up to 9.3 miles. He told me he stopped in between the loops and sat and meditated. Again, I was impressed. I was proud of him for taking care of himself, even if he didn't want to discuss his process with me. It felt like it was a very private process, and I honored that. I learned later that he wasn't really running or meditating. Silly me. But at the time, I believed him. I held the fort down at home and many nights, he came home late. Sometimes 11:00 p.m. I supported him because he had supported me through all of my marathon training and meditation retreats. And I wanted to do the same for him. Besides, that is what you do for someone you love. You support them. I told him not to worry about the kids. *I've got them.*

I remember sitting with a friend and telling her how proud I was of Jeff for all the work he was doing on himself. As I told her everything he was doing and how late he was coming home from work, her smile dipped a little and her eyes showed disbelief. She quickly tried to cover the look up. She was savvier to life and recognized the signs of something not adding up. I would find out later that she suspected he was up to no good.

* * *

During our marriage, I had recurrent dreams of people coming to my home and trying to invade it. In each of these dreams, I was alone, trying to keep them out. I was trying to protect my children and my home. My husband at the time was nowhere to be found. Each time I had this dream, I woke up sweating. My whole sense of safety and stability were shaken for a few days.

Back then, I had no idea what these dreams meant.

Over the course of a few years, as the dreams continued, things started falling into place. One morning during the summer of 2008, I was awakened at 8:00 a.m. by pounding on my front door. I froze for a second. The pounding continued. It reminded me of the multiple dreams I had had where someone was trying to get into my house, but I was trying to push them out or keep them from getting in. I lay there in bed, hoping that my husband was downstairs and would handle it. But the pounding continued. My husband had gone somewhere, and I was home alone with my four sleeping kids. My heart raced. I hoped he would just go away. But alas he didn't. The pounding continued.

I reluctantly went downstairs, eyeing the bow staff that I kept at the front door. As a second-degree brown belt, I knew how to use it, so it made me feel a little better. I looked through the window and saw a big man standing there with a visibly annoyed look on his face. I opened the door about two inches and asked him what he wanted. He told me he was there for my moving sale. *Uh…moving sale?* I was confused. When I told him there was no sale, he started yelling at me, telling me he drove an hour to get to my house that morning. I was confused and a bit unnerved. It took several minutes before I convinced him that there was no moving sale at my home. He pulled out an advertisement he had clipped, which sure enough, had my address and a big listing that said "moving, everything must go CHEAP." Throughout that day, I had a parade of people coming to my front door for the big sale.

This was one of those scenarios that totally played out the recurrent dreams I had been having. The dreams continued. More vivid, more strangers trying to invade my home, and me with my kids, husband nowhere in sight.

The reason I bring this up is that for years, I had these dreams. And for years, I suspected they were signs from the Universe, but I had no idea what they meant.

I was no stranger to my dreams being indicators of events that were happening or were about to happen. I don't know if it is called intuition, clairvoyance, or premonitions. Maybe it was a combination of the three that warned me or brought my attention to things I needed to know. I wasn't entirely cognizant of what it all meant, but I started to view these things as one of my most precious gifts.

The first time I really noticed it was when I was well into my second year of pharmacy school when I had a vivid dream about my friend being badly injured. When I called him a few weeks later to check in on him, he told me he had been in a terrible accident in upstate Wisconsin and had been in the hospital around the time I had the dream.

I was also very in tune with signs from the Universe and looked for their meaning when they arrived. One beautiful summer evening, my kids were playing in the backyard, and I was grilling salmon on the deck. I stood next to the grill, holding the spatula, looking at the vibrant green leaves on the trees and noticing the bright blue sky and the white puffy clouds that reminded me of Teletubbies. I had a smile on my face as I watched my kids run around joyfully. Just then, a beautiful monarch butterfly landed on my hand. It sat there for the longest time. The spatula was in my hand, but I just stopped everything and stood still. I breathed it in. I had a sense of knowing in my heart. A sense of peaceful reassurance. I literally felt the love and support of the Universe shining down on me.

I looked at my husband, who was standing right next to me and said, "There is something really BIG going on, and this butterfly is telling me that whatever it is, I will be okay."

I swear he must have been pissing his pants as I was saying this.

Chapter 4

The First Big Reveal

WE HAD A WONDERFUL TIME on Labor Day weekend in Cook's Forest, Pennsylvania. It was an annual event. We took the kids canoeing down the Clarion River and stayed at a lodge along the river. At some point, we took the kids to play Putt-Putt golf and eat Big Macs from McDonald's. That was a rare event because we didn't eat fast food but a few times a year. On the day of the reunion, we spent the whole day watching the kids playing in the creek and mud, hiking, eating a ton of food, and talking and laughing with Jeff's extended family.

We loved our long weekends because as business owners, it was rare to have one. We took advantage of any days off where we didn't have to be at the pharmacy.

But this weekend was different. When we came home, Jeff told me he was going to work. *That's odd,* I thought. *We never go to work on a holiday weekend.*

By the time 9:00 p.m. came around, the kids were in bed, and I had a little time to myself. I was confused about why Jeff had gone into work and not continued our family time. And then I remembered. I had wanted to check his phone records two months ago after our trip to Washington, DC. This was a good time to do that.

I sat down at my computer and logged into my account. When I clicked on the detailed listing of text messages, I could not believe what I was seeing. There were over two thousand text messages at all hours of the day to one phone number. In just the past month. I quickly did a reverse phone search to find that he had been texting a former girlfriend from high school. One who had also surprised him by randomly showing up to his apartment while we were in pharmacy school. One, who when I showed up to the apartment on her surprise visit, was quick to tell me she was engaged and shoved her ring in my face. The whole interaction, as I remembered it, was very odd.

I printed out the log of text messages. And I called my sister-in-law/best friend/soul sister, Liz. It was 11:00 p.m. by now. Jeff still wasn't home. I started telling Liz about the text messages. I was sure there was something going on. She agreed. As I cried, I asked, "Do you think they've held hands?!"

Do you think they've held hands?!

When Liz heard those words, she pulled the phone away from her face and looked at it with eyes wide open. Her jaw dropped as she silently mouthed the words, "Oh. My. God."

This is when she knew that she had to go slow with me. I was devastated at the mere thought that my husband could be holding hands with someone else. Even though I was forty-one years old and a mother of four children, it never crossed my mind that my husband would do more than hold hands with another woman. Liz treaded lightly with me. My brother, Sam, got on the phone and told me we would figure this out. That I didn't have to stay with Jeff. That money wasn't an issue, and I had their total emotional support.

This comforted me.

The next day, September 9, 2009, at 9:00 a.m., I called Jeff at work. I confronted him. This is when I learned that he and she had, in fact, held hands. And a whole lot more. Okay, now THIS was devastating. I called Liz as I lay on the floor in fetal position, repeating over and over, "I need you."

I feel like it is my duty to help you understand who you are reading about. I wouldn't be surprised if you were sitting there shaking your head in disbelief at the level of my naivety. I would if I were you. So let me go back much further.

CHAPTER 5

ME

EVER SINCE I CAN REMEMBER, I have dreamed about having a deeply loving relationship with a beautiful man, inside and out. I was boy crazy from the time I was in first grade. That phase never ended. When I set my eyes on a boy, I became devoted to him. As I got older, I continued this pattern.

I grew up in both Indian culture and American culture— somewhere in there, I suppose. It was confusing to say the least, especially when it came to relationships. I was always privy to the conversations my mom had with her friends. They often spoke about people they knew in India and the gossip that was coming down the pike. I can remember the undertones of shame in their voices as they talked about a girl leaving the village to have a "love marriage." *God forbid. A woman chose to leave the village and avoid an arranged marriage because she fell in love. What the hell was wrong with her?* They always whispered the part where they said, "love marriage," as if it was the most shameful thing in the world. I heard their messages loud and clear.

The patriarchy in India is alive and well, as it is in other countries like the US. My dad came to the United States in 1965, and my mom followed two years later. India seemed to be about fifty years behind us in terms of social acceptance of love and affection. Even though the years were passing and the people in India were becoming more accepting of dating and love relationships, it was as if time stood still in our home. As far as relationships went, I grew up with the same cultural expectations my parents knew when they were growing up in the 1940s and 1950s.

When I was an early teen, as my body started changing and developing, I hid aspects of it to avoid bringing my femininity out into the open where everyone could see. I had been conditioned to feel shame for my female body and anything associated with sex. When I started dating in high school, my family gave me looks of shame if I sat too close to my boyfriend. I quickly learned that it was not okay to show affection because I would be labeled as cheap. No respectable man would want to marry me if I was dirty in any way. And in our house, what society thought of us meant everything. Sadly, this ruled many of my thoughts and decisions.

This concept didn't jibe with the fact that the *Kama Sutra* originated in India, and they have an overwhelming problem with overpopulation. But I let the idea that the female body was meant to be covered up sink into me. Sex was something that was dirty. Anything associated with sex was shameful. Periods were dirty. And pregnancy was too. When I was finally carrying my first baby to term after three years of infertility and a miscarriage, I joyfully mentioned that she was kicking. They responded with a look of shame.

Outward affection was not shown in my home growing up. It was not part of the culture. My mom grew up in a small village in India. Her mom was very strict and made sure that she raised her daughter with impeccable Indian values. The kind of girl who could attract a good husband. When my mom was sixteen years old, she was arranged to wed my dad, who was twenty-one. They called him a "diamond." He was a handsome young man with fair skin. He was highly educated and at the top of his class. He was going places. He even spoke English. Score. Her parents then made it their mission to make sure she was well prepared to be a good Indian wife who cooked great meals and tended to the needs of the home. My parents might have seen each other a handful of times over the next five years before they married. They didn't know each other as friends. They knew each other as the person they would wed and start a family with. They would continue with the traditions and cultural expectations set out by their parents.

While I was growing up, everything my parents did was for the family unit. My mom sent her salary back to India to help the family. My dad worked hard to bring his family and hundreds of others from the villages in India to the United States for a better life of opportunity. Education was a big deal. The value of sacrificing for the family was deeply ingrained in me. Anything for the family unit, and especially when there are kids involved. I never saw divorce, and everything that was modeled to me was loyalty to family and a utilitarian relationship where there is division of labor, and everyone pitches in. The biggest sacrifices are made for others, even if it was at the expense of individual happiness. Interdependence versus independence. What society thinks matters. Family is everything.

I suppose both nature and nurture were involved with what formed me. I learned to be self-sacrificing, a people pleaser, and a conflict avoider. I learned to silently suffer and to put on a happy face even in the face of the darkest adversity. I learned not to talk about the problems of my life and to not air dirty laundry. I learned to protect the reputation of people around me at all costs. So, the transgressions that my partners may have had were for me to keep to myself. I put on a happy and "on top of the world" facade through any hardship. I only talked about my hardships once I came out the other end, successful in my triumph and finding a reason for why I went through it. I have used my adversity every step of the way to help ease others' suffering. My ability to "keep rising" comes from my mom. "Everything happens for a reason" was something my mom repeatedly said in her own language, Gujarati, and it resonated within my soul. I knew that if I kept walking the path, I would walk long enough for *A* reason to reveal itself. Sometimes it felt like a reason would never emerge. But years down the line, after a devastating event, the reason would emerge, and I could find an opportunity for growth.

At the same time, I learned to be compassionate and to hear the cries of those who are suffering. I could rationalize anyone's poor behavior. As a Libra, I could see all sides of a situation or issue. I remember crying to my boyfriend in college about how I had no opinions. The people around me were having extensive conversations about politics and religion, and I simply had no opinion one way or the other. I could see both sides. I could see how people's upbringing or specific interests would have them lean one way or another politically. And neither side was wrong. It just was what it was. And my insecurities and people pleasing tendencies made me hesitant to speak out loud if I did have an opinion because I didn't want to upset anyone. I sat, silencing myself. I didn't even know I was doing that.

When someone wronged me, I looked at the situation and worked to understand why they might act in a certain way. As I encountered more and more people who were flawed or had wounds, I decided it was my job to help fix them. Or at least influence them to fix themselves. This wasn't a decision I was conscious of. I just did it. It felt good.

I think if you asked people how they viewed me, they would give you a very different answer than what I would give. I didn't quite *believe in* my worth. But I came off as confident, a go-getter, always happy, successful, and like I had no real problems in life. But just because I didn't talk about them didn't mean I didn't have them. I had my fair share. I was just taught not to talk about them to the outside world. There was a sense of shame in letting people know everything wasn't perfect. I didn't understand, at the time, that my parents grew up in a tiny village in India, where everyone knew everyone else's business. If someone had an issue or a problem, the whole village knew about it. Gossip spread like wildfire, and to avoid being the subject of it, it was best to not expose yourself.

Also growing up, I did not see intimacy, love, hugs, or affection. I saw my mom going to work, my dad going to work, my mom cooking dinner for us, watching the news with my dad, doing some fun stuff as a family, then going to sleep. I did not receive "I love you's," as it just wasn't a part of our culture. Love was shown in other ways. In providing for us, in spending time with us, teaching us, and being consistently there.

As a child, I was one of the most emotional, sensitive creatures that I knew. But I was taught that emotions would get me nowhere, so I hid them. I worked hard to not show people that I was even remotely affected by anything sensitive. I grew to be ashamed of tears that would well up when I was touched by a commercial or by the display of a human being reaching out to another human being in need. I didn't feel comfortable in my own skin to cry in public when someone was hurt or suffering. I didn't feel comfortable to even cry in front of my own children when I was so deeply touched at a school assembly. I would laugh and think of something to divert my focus from experiencing an emotional moment. I thought less of myself because of how many times I had to work to tamp down my emotions. Emotions would get me nowhere. Especially not emotional reactions to things happening around me or an honest expression of how I felt about something "controversial." It was through my analytical, rational, and scientific mind that I would achieve success. And success in my academic and professional life would yield happiness for years to come. After all, if I am accomplished in that arena, then how could I ever want for more? HA. It amazes me how much of the human experience I missed out on—I used that energy to suppress my emotions.

I fulfilled my need for emotional and psychological depth by surrounding myself with people who needed help. As it turns out, I was naturally gifted at soothing people who were suffering. I didn't quite know this. I needed external validation at that point in my life, and for years to come before I started to see and know my gift for myself.

I attracted all sorts of people in need. Including love interests. In my quest for connection, I had countless coffee dates that were "all about them." Even though I was always the one reaching out, when I got there, the person sitting across from me took over most of the conversation by prattling on endlessly about their various life problems. I had lots of social engagements, but very few were fulfilling to me. They were more or less opportunities for me to be around people and not alone.

I didn't know there was a difference between being alone and being lonely. I thought that it would be enough to just listen to others talk about their problems or challenges. Though it never quite satisfied my yearning for connection, I confused people talking TO me with connection. Even though I was not alone, the interactions with these self-absorbed people drained me. No one ever asked about me. And if they did, I would get one sentence out before the topic was drawn back to them. This, in effect, reinforced my belief that what I had to say was not important to others. I learned that people were inherently not interested in me, my fears, my needs, my likes and dislikes. I continued to silence myself. Throughout this period of my life, my life force was dwindling, but my deep longing for authentic connection continued. I just couldn't clearly articulate what it was that was missing from my life. I didn't have the language and awareness to do so.

Theoretically, in the way I was raised, surface relationships should have been enough. But not for me. I wanted so badly to be in love and to have someone to be in love with me. I wanted to feel special. And adored. I wanted so much to be comfortable enough in my own skin to feel and express emotions and own them. I wanted to have opinions and to have people find me interesting. I wanted validation for everything that was going on inside of my mind. I longed to be understood. These burning desires lay suppressed inside of me for years, but inevitably came out. Fires that are smoldering inside of a spiritual being cannot be suppressed. They are meant to burn hot, and when the perfect catalyst presents itself, the Universe will make sure that it burns bright one way or another. As it turns out for me, one devastating life event after another paved the path for my perfect evolution. Each of these life events would fan a little more air onto the embers within me.

Ultimately, though, when I chose to marry the first time at the age of twenty-four, I chose a life similar to that which was modeled for me. I chose "safe." I chose utilitarian. I chose what I thought was stable. It was not unlike the Indian model of marriage; except I was best friends with my husband. We had what seemed like a full, devoted life. I didn't know anything different. We both had the same professional and family goals. We worked together, and we raised our family together. It seemed to flow effortlessly with the division of labor that we had adopted and with the shared values I thought we had.

You can imagine my surprise when I learned that my husband was cheating on me twenty-one years into our relationship.

Just recently, my girls were calling me out on just how naive I have been over the years. My oldest daughter has told me several times that I am the most naive person she has ever met. And she wondered how I could be so naive and trusting after experiencing the shitty experiences I have had in life. She reminded me about the time that I had befriended a local schoolteacher. Whenever I saw him out and about, which was often back then, I said hi, gave hugs to everyone with him, and engaged in chitchat. My daughter recalled one evening after the Fourth of July fireworks, when I had about ten kids at our home. I had been texting with this younger man and invited him over to hang out. It was midnight. He came over, had a mango shake (ha-ha), talked for a while, and then left after about an hour. I didn't think anything of it. But I learned, much later, that when I invited him over, he thought it was for a booty call. I laugh at the hilarity of it. Because my head just doesn't think that way. I don't go there, and I don't assume that a man I have befriended has those thoughts about me. Yeah, I know. It's hard to believe anyone could be this naive. 1 am living proof. And yet, somehow, I still function and thrive as a human being in this world.

I see the world from a place of innocence of a five-year-old girl. I love that place. It is a happy, joyful, uncomplicated place. I CHOOSE to live in that space as much as I can. Life is complicated enough. I don't want to have to be on high alert all the time or think the worst of people. I don't want to live in a place where I can't just take people at face value. So, if being naive and innocent means that, then I will continue to choose that.

It is not like I am unaware of the fact that sometimes life on the outside is seemingly evil, or that shit happens. It is just that I choose to reside in my world of butterflies and rainbows because it feels better to me. It feels better than being cynical and bitter, always waiting for the other shoe to drop. I like innocence, and if there is ever a time I can return to innocence, that would be my most cherished desire.

I sometimes assume that others live with that same sense of innocence as me, and that is where I run into challenges. As my first marriage was ending, I was thinking about my life ahead and came to a realization I shared with Liz. I told her that as compassionate as I am, and as many angles I can see someone's problems or issues from, that whenever I started dating, I was bound to get screwed over. The simple solution to this was to not date.

Regarding my first marriage ending, though, I had no idea how much of the Indian culture was ingrained in me and how much cultural expectations and societal norms were a part of my psyche. I was willing to do whatever was necessary to preserve the family unit. When I was growing up, the stereotype was that kids who came from divorced families didn't fare too well. And my kids meant everything to me. So, if it meant that I would live out this lifetime in a loveless, unfaithful marriage, I could put a smile on my face and find fulfillment through my children. I had seen this done in countless families before, and I was more than capable of accomplishing this great feat. I mistakenly thought that a family needed two parents, even if they were unhappy. I didn't realize until later that two miserable parents would make for kids who didn't fare so well, and that having one happy parent was much better for the kids.

At the time, I thought I could pull off the charade. I thought that my love and devotion to my children could power me through anything. But my inner spirit wouldn't allow it. I was meant for greater things. I was meant for a greater love. I needed to continue to evolve into the empowered woman I was meant to be. I had a range of emotions and depth of feelings that I had yet to discover.

The fiery rage that was ignited within me from Jeff's affair didn't allow for me to continue silencing myself enough to make our home environment acceptable for him. He didn't play by the same cultural rules I played. He found my anger and the fire within me to be intolerable, and he chose to leave the marriage four short months after his affair came to light. Thank goodness.

Moving forward, I intentionally decided that I would no longer allow my cultural upbringing to hold me back in the way of expressing myself, of displaying affection, of holding hands or hugging my man in front of my parents. I decided I would start crying in front of people and own my emotions.

When he left, I felt like a gigantic weight had been lifted off me. It gave me a second chance in this lifetime. It gave me the courage to love deeper than I have ever loved. It gave me a chance to experience deeper emotions across the board than I could have ever imagined. It allowed me the freedom to spread my wings and start walking in the direction of who I was supposed to become this lifetime. It gave me the opportunity to tap into my vast amount of gifts to share with people around me. And to have the confidence in myself to be able to do so. It gave me a glimpse of what it felt like to start using my voice. And I was able to finally release unfulfilling relationships and form the connections that would satisfy my deep longing for love and belonging in a soulmate sort of way.

But it didn't all happen once he left. No, I needed another catalyst to help me along. I needed more life experiences to get me to a point where I would ultimately choose me. And for those catalysts, a.k.a. really shitty life moments, I am ever so thankful.

Chapter 6

Serendipity

OVER THE FALL 2009 SOCCER season, I dragged myself to the soccer fields and took my son to practice. I walked around the fields talking on the phone and crying about my marriage falling apart while I watched the boys practice. I wouldn't get too close to anyone because I didn't want them to see me crying. But also, the only time I had to talk on the phone about all the details was while I was at soccer practice. This was my ME time. No listening ears of my children, and I could let it all out. By now, my son had a new coach. But his age group practiced at the same time as other team levels of the same age group. So sometimes, I would randomly see his former coach across the field.

That sweet man would always wave from a distance or shout from a distance, "How are you?" And I would say," Great! How are you?" That was it. I would shake my head because I couldn't, for the life of me, remember his name. I was thankful that he was always a distance away, so I wouldn't be put into the awkward position of having to ask him his name again. I knew it was something simple with one syllable, but I was too embarrassed to ask. And plus, given my distraught emotional state, it was best to just keep my distance.

When Jeff moved out on January 10, 2010, I vowed to myself and to my friends that I would not date until my children had graduated from high school and were in college. My sole purpose was to raise them, so they felt love, were well adjusted, and had bright futures. It didn't occur to me that I would ever want to date.

I attended a Chopra Center meditation retreat in Marco Island, Florida, that March and befriended a group of fellow meditators. I sat on the beach one evening, after sunset yoga, talking with one of my new friends. I told him about my impending divorce and how wonderful my children were. I told him of my plans to not date for the next ten years. I told him I didn't need that.

I can still hear his response in my mind.

"You deserve to love and to be loved. You deserve to feel special and have someone dote over you. You deserve to be happy and experience all of that. Don't sell yourself short, and don't rob yourself of that experience."

At the time, I shrugged it off. *Clearly, he doesn't understand,* I thought to myself. But his words were like seeds that had been planted in fertile soil. As time passed, they would take hold and grow roots.

It was at that same meditation retreat that I asked one of the lead speakers and motivators of the event, Davidji if he had some time to talk. I had met Davidji at my very first Chopra Center event in 2007, and he was one of my gurus. I told him that I was struggling with a major life event, and I couldn't quite make sense of it or get to a point where I could accept it. He graciously obliged. I told him the story about my husband, our kids, his affair, and him moving out. I told Davidji, "He left me."

After offering his compassion, empathy, and love, he responded with some very wise words.

"Maybe you can think about it a little differently. Men are constantly distracted by shiny objects. The other woman was just another shiny object. Don't judge the shiny object because you may also be a shiny object at some point. Rather than telling your story that he left you, maybe you can change that to *he changed his mind.* Have you ever changed your mind?"

I thought to myself, *yes, I have changed my mind plenty of times.*

HUGE mindset shift.

There was a lot to process. I wasn't processing a broken heart. I was processing a broken marriage. A broken partnership.

Fall soccer season 2010 eventually arrived, and I had had a few distant encounters with my son's former coach, a.k.a. Coach Eye Candy. I was feeling well adjusted since Jeff moved out, and I was moving on with my life. I was completely devoted to being a mom of four kids and loving our lives together. Let me make it perfectly clear: I had no intentions of dating. I was not looking for a man. I was not interested in a man. I did not need a man in my life. Those sentences became my mantra anytime anyone asked.

It was a fateful day at the beginning of September when our team won a game, and Coach Eye Candy's team also won a game. The tradition was to get ice cream at the local custard stand after the game. So, our two respective teams happened to be there at the same time.

I picked up my cone and was walking with our coach, Susan, and another mom. As we made our way from the front of the ice cream stand to meet the boys at the back of the parking lot, Coach Eye Candy walked across the driveway. He firmly shook my hand, looked into my eyes, and said, "Hi Sujata. How are you?" I nearly melted.

Impressed at the firm grip of his handshake, I shook back and said with a big smile, "I'm great! How are you?" He must have responded he was doing well also. And as quickly as he appeared, he retreated back to his team.

I slowly walked with Susan, who happened to be a mutual friend. "What is his name?" I asked.

"Nick," she replied.

Ahhh! Nick! Yes, simple, one syllable. Nick.

I casually said, "He seems like a nice guy. Is he single?"

"Yes, actually he is," she said matter-of-factly.

I quickly shot back, "Oh never mind. I don't actually care. I don't want a man. I don't need a man. I am not dating for another ten years when my children graduate from high school."

To this day, she still laughs at the fact that I said that.

But something in me couldn't stop there.

"Wait a minute. Why is he single? Because if he is single for the same reason Jeff is single, I don't want anything to do with him!"

Susan responded with, "Well, actually, his wife left him—for another woman."

Oh man. Why did you tell me that? That is completely devastating! That poor guy! Now you're tugging on my heart strings. I love to be there for people who are suffering! Remember how I fulfill my psychological needs? This is my gift!

So, I followed that surprising revelation with, "Okay, well IF he happens to want to have coffee because he needs a friend, I would be happy to do that. But only coffee. Poor guy."

I was acting as if he would even be interested in dating me.

My next question was, "How many kids does he have?"

"Three boys," she responded.

"Oh, hell no! I don't want to date anyone with kids."

At which point, the other mom we were walking with chimed in, "Sujata, you want someone who has kids because he'll understand you being a mom more than someone who doesn't have kids."

I didn't buy it. Life was complicated enough as it was. I was going through my divorce, adjusting to life with a couple of middle-schoolers and lots of athletic activities and homework. I didn't need any potential stressors added to the mix.

I ended the conversation with something to the effect that I would gladly be a friend but nothing more.

Sure, Sujata.

My intention was to only be a friend. But now Nick was in my awareness and had my attention. The next time I was at the field, I noticed everything about him. He was throwing a football around with his son. I noticed his amazing calves and his well-defined pecs through his fitted T-shirt. I could not stop looking at him. His biceps and triceps as he threw and caught the ball, his dark complexion, his gorgeous smile. I noticed how energetic he was, how encouraging he was to his son, how hot he looked. *Damn it! This may thwart my plan of celibacy.*

Ultimately, Susan told him that I had asked about him. He didn't know I was single and asked her why she hadn't told him before. She told him that I was going through a lot and didn't need him bothering me. As Susan relayed to me later, his response to her about me was, "She's the shit!" He later told me that he wanted to jump up and down when he learned that I was asking about him. Of course he did! Who wouldn't?

Susan asked me if she could share my phone number with him if he asked for it, and I casually said, "Sure."

Let me backtrack a little here. Because I think it is really cool how the numbers and stars lined up along this path. Going back to finding out my ex-husband was cheating on me. It was September 9, 2009, at 9:00 a.m. (9/9/09, 9am). Look at all those nines! By the time I was asking Susan about Nick, it was the week before the anniversary of the big reveal with Jeff. It had been an especially emotional year, and my primary goal was to make sure my kiddos adjusted well to the change in our family structure. As for me, I asked the Universe to replace the memory of what I learned a year ago with something good. It is common for traumatic events to be felt at the anniversaries of those events, even subconsciously. And it really was devastating to me a year ago. So, I wanted to replace that memory with something not so traumatic. I didn't want my body to go through that experience year after year. I asked the Universe for it. Very clearly.

The morning of September 9, 2010, my two older kids had just left for school. I was homeschooling my two youngest children, and they were still asleep. I received a text message on my heavy-duty flip phone. I flipped it open and saw that it was from Nick. He messaged how thrilled he was to learn that I was single and was sorry that I was going through whatever pain I might be going through. I don't remember the exact words, but I remember feeling like I was reading something I would have written.

It was a year to the date of me finding out about Jeff's affair—a week after I asked the Universe for something to replace the traumatic revelation…THIS.

It was before 7:30 a.m., and my heart started beating out of my chest just reading this text. Coach Eye Candy was texting me and giving me attention! I must have texted him back a thank you and some other random things I can't remember. And then I immediately called Liz.

"This hot guy from the soccer fields texted me!" I exclaimed.

At that moment, my call waiting beeped. I looked at the caller ID and it was HIM!

"WTF?! Why is he calling me?! I don't know how to talk to a man!! Oh my God. What do I do?" I panicked.

I let it go to voice mail while Liz and I came up with my next best step. I called him back. Novel approach.

From the moment we started talking, we connected in a crazy, universal, soulmate kind of way. It was so easy to talk with him. His voice, his inquisitiveness, his interest in me. He was open. He talked about himself but not to the point of annoyance. Just enough to share. We started right off the bat with deep topics. There was a healthy give and take. I felt like we had known each other before. In another lifetime. He felt like a comfortable home to me.

My heart was totally fluttering. I couldn't wipe the schoolgirl smile off my face. This guy lit me up.

It just so happened that he was leaving town for a conference in Washington, DC, but that day and every day while he was away, he texted me in the morning and sent me multiple messages throughout the day. His messages sounded like he was falling for me. He even sent me the lyrics to a song that revealed some deep love for me, even though we had just started talking. As it turns out, he mistakenly sent the wrong lyrics. He had meant to send me the lyrics to Fleetwood Mac's "You Make Lovin' Fun." But he inadvertently sent me lyrics to a song by a Christian singer that professed a deep love. We would laugh at that later. But I do believe there are no accidents. I am convinced he was falling for me. Just as I was for him.

When his meetings were over each day and my kids were asleep, I would get butterflies in my stomach as I waited for him to call me. We talked for hours and hours. I remember lying on my bathroom floor with my feet up on the garden tub, laughing, sharing, and my heart beating a million beats per minute. We were so aligned that at one point I asked him if he was mocking me. His language pattern was so similar to mine. But he said that is just the way he talks. One more thing we shared. He seemed, in those countless hours that we talked, like the male version of me.

With each conversation, our connection grew. I thought about him incessantly, and he said the same about me. We learned more and more about things we had in common. This man paying attention to me and showing interest in me was capturing my heart. But the things we had in common and how easy it was to talk with him made me start to think that maybe, just maybe—I could date him.

CHAPTER 7

OUR EARLY, CONFUSING DAYS

NICK AND I TALKED ON the phone every day while he was on his trip, multiple times a day. We were setting the foundations of whatever would come. We were both excited that we would soon get to see each other and connect in person.

It was a beautiful fall Monday. He was driving home from Washington, D.C, and we were getting together at 6:00 p.m. He would be worn out for sure after a conference and all the driving. So, we agreed I would meet him at his house. We could sit on his side yard patio and go for a walk if we felt like it. This served me quite well because I could not fathom going out and eating a meal with him. My stomach was full of butterflies, and we really didn't want anyone else around the love fest that was well under way. We wanted to continue to connect and get to know each other even better.

I spent the afternoon going through my closet and picking out an outfit that was casual and reflected who I was as a person, but also not so casual that I was sending the message that I didn't care. I settled on a khaki miniskirt to highlight my legs and a black top that had a lotus on the back with the word "peace" underneath it. I waited until late afternoon to jump into the shower and then did my hair extra special. I felt pretty.

I had driven past his house a day earlier to check it out, so I knew where it was. I was also curious about where he lived. Susan had told me his house was "cute," so I had to see it for myself in advance of our date.

The evening we were supposed to meet, I pulled into his driveway just in time for him to be walking out the front door and making his way toward me. He had a pair of faded jeans on and was barefoot. He wore a snug-fitting T-shirt that showed off his very well-developed pecs. I nervously opened my car door, got out, and walked toward him. I walked to his outstretched arms for what I thought was going to be a "welcome home" hug. I thought a hug was the most appropriate, considering how much we had connected over the past few days. And considering how naive and new I was to this whole dating thing, a warm hug seemed pretty forward to me.

But he went in for a kiss. An awkward kiss. It really took me by surprise and wasn't exactly the way I wanted our first kiss to be. It didn't feel romantic or like the culmination of serious connecting and looking into each other's eyes. I know, I have my dreams. In my fantasy world, I had envisioned sitting on the side patio, talking about all things, realizing we were soulmates who had finally found each other in this lifetime while we gazed into each other's eyes. We would have no other choice but to seal our long-awaited journey back to each other with a magical kiss, with fireworks above us, butterflies fluttering around, birds strewing popcorn and cranberry garlands on the evergreen trees, and triumphant music playing in the background. It would be the kiss of all kisses. The divine energy that connected us, our union orchestrated by the Universe, would be able to be felt for miles around us.

A girl can dream.

The awkward kiss was followed by pleasantries as we walked into his house. He showed me around, and then we sat down on his only piece of sit-down furniture in his living room, an old, yellow plaid loveseat. His anxiety was palpable. His face was quivering, and he had a noticeable shakiness and strain in his voice. His eyes were red, likely from the late nights of talking and the long drive home. They looked like he had so much he needed to tell me. But he seemed almost afraid.

One of my self-proclaimed superpowers is that I can use my calming energy to help soothe others. I suggested we go for a walk around the block so we could breathe in the autumn air and talk. We stopped on the bleachers at the park at the end of his street and sat down for a brief time. He had some things he wanted to tell me. Personal things that he thought might be a dealbreaker for me. Well, my dear, that is not the way I work. I am an information gatherer. I gather information without all my emotions attached to it. And then when it is a convenient time for me, I analyze the data and form a conclusion.

I have a great ability to do that repeatedly with all sorts of life-changing events. Gather the information, put it all in one place, then sit down and look at it. Ask for clarity, meditate, sleep on it, and then make decisions whenever I feel like I have come to a place of peace about it. That's me.

We continued our walk, and we talked about all sorts of things. At one point, we stopped, and I hugged him so I could breathe with him to bring some calming energy into our evening.

Our date ended at 1:00 a.m. It was a late night. There was a lot of talking, and a lot of not talking. I was on cloud nine for some parts of it and confused about other parts of it. One of the things that stuck out to me was something he said to me when we were on our walk around the block.

He pointed to his head with his lips quivering and mouthed, "I'm still fucked up in here." (No worries, I can help fix that!).

Let's just say I gathered a lot of information that night, and I had a lot of analyzing to do. I had no idea what this meant or what it would mean for me in the coming months and years.

Those very early days of us dating were confusing at best. Actually, we went from this soulmate, fireworks connection to a roller coaster ride I hadn't planned on. Nine days after our first date, I came bouncing over to his house to see him. We sat down on the plaid love seat, and he started telling me how amazing I was.

WOW, I thought, *this guy digs me!*

And then he ended the scroll of compliments with, "I can't see you anymore."

Uh…. excuse me?! What just happened?!

He didn't say anything that made sense to me. Nothing seemed logical. I left there completely confused.

But he couldn't stop calling me.

I remembered that he had given me full disclosure that he was still fucked up in the head. I understand what it feels like to be wounded and still want a better life for yourself. I understand not having the tools to process life events, and I also understood that I felt I had the unique gifts to support him through it. I felt like we had made a promise to each other in another lifetime to find each other and heal old wounds in this lifetime. I don't know why I was so resolved to this notion. It is not something I thought up in my mind. It was something I KNEW in the deep recesses of my body and soul.

So that week, we went out on another date. That lasted another month or so until he started feeling close to me, and then he broke up with me again. On that same yellow plaid love seat, which from that moment forward I refused to sit on, as I labeled it the breakup couch. It felt like he was scared. Afraid of missing out on something better, or just afraid of true intimacy. Or both.

Along with his on-again, off-again behavior, he was extremely defensive. I can't remember the specifics of any particular conversation, but his patterns of defensiveness certainly revealed themselves over certain issues. I know it comes from feelings of not being good enough or unworthiness. And I suspect it came from his upbringing in a world where he did not feel important. I still recall the night we sat out in the rain in the parking lot of a local pub. I told him I was OUT. I couldn't take his defensiveness to simple things anymore. I had four kids I was raising, and I knew who I was. I did not need to be in a relationship with someone who was this defensive and could not have a conversation about simple things. (God, I love empowered and confident Sujata!)

He responded with tears. He cried and kept telling me he would do better. I had never dealt with anything like this before. I had never had a man plead with me to give him another chance to do better. With me, what you see is what you get. If there is something I need to work on, I identify it and then get to work. And that's how I transform areas of my life for the better. From my naive, trusting soul, when he promised he would do better and not be defensive, I believed him. I also believed that he had the awareness and the tools to do the work quickly and seamlessly. This, combined with my compassionate heart and remembering him pointing to his head saying, "I am still fucked up in here," kept me answering the phone when he called.

For some reason, whenever we got close, it triggered something in him that seemed to scare him. And he would retreat. It felt like the classic avoidant attachment style typical of someone who had been abandoned early in life. A fear of intimacy. (For more information on attachment styles, I highly recommend the book *Attached* by Amir Levine and Rachel Heller.) As I looked back on this years later, I had no idea how difficult it would be to navigate the avoidant attachment style, and more importantly, that it would take me from a somewhat secure attachment style to a very anxious one. But at the time, recognizing that pattern, in early November, I suggested we just be friends.

I still felt a huge connection to him, and I knew he felt it with me. But something between us wasn't going to work out as a couple because there was a lot of damage from his upbringing, from a past life, or from a previous marriage. At the time, I didn't quite know the extent of his dysfunction, inner child wounds, abandonment, avoidant attachment style, and so much more. I had no idea how long it would take to unpack all of these wounds for him to heal and feel whole.

But this book isn't about how he healed. This is about my journey.

When we decided to be "just friends," it felt like a huge weight had been lifted off me. I could be me. Just wonderful, authentic me. There was no pressure to be anything else. It was comfortable, and there was no pressure on him either.

Nick and I continued our friendship. We were connected on so many levels. Our conversations lasted for hours. We couldn't wait to see each other each day. He called me on his way to and from work every single day. We met up in the mornings at 5:00 a.m. for a spin class and sometimes had coffee afterward. I am not a morning person. For me to get up and go anywhere by 5:00 a.m. is a huge statement as to where my heart lies.

We had plenty of dinners together as a couple and also with all of our kids together. The two of us took a trip to Cincinnati to go to his godson's musical, and we had a blast driving down and back. We were light-hearted and silly. We talked about anything and everything. We blasted the music really loud, and he simulated being a part of the band as we cruised down the highway. We sang familiar tunes at the top of our lungs. We laughed so much I can still remember my belly hurting from laughing so hard. I clearly had feelings for him, and he had feelings for me. But we kept it at a friend level for almost two months.

As winter rolled around and school was called off for snow days, his kids came over and spent the day with mine. I took them sled riding, to the stores, and out to breakfast. I cooked dinner for our combined families, and Nick came to my house right after work for a big family dinner and to retrieve his sons. It felt good. We were a bit touchy feely with one another, which was confusing for me as well as some of our kids. But during this time, our friendship flourished and grew stronger.

Sometime in the middle of December, we were talking on the phone. I was driving down the main street in our town during rush hour traffic. I remember sitting at the traffic light when Nick told me he loved me. I looked at my phone as if to make sure it was Nick that I was talking to. I thought maybe he said it inadvertently. I didn't say it back. I wasn't sure if I should call attention to it or let it go. Later he asked me how I felt about his professed love for me.

That Christmas Eve, Nick came over and brought me a gift. We ended up talking and getting back together as a couple that day.

A few weeks later, we were off again. Oh. My. God! I was DONE.

Until he came knocking on my door, begging for me to give him one more chance. I know, I know… I can hear you all now telling me to run…my former self even still tells me to run. But alas, I did not.

Some might consider all of these as red flags. In my clouded judgment, I did not see them. Or maybe I did but didn't allow myself to act on them. I had never been in a situation like this before. When someone pled with me for forgiveness or a second chance, I gave second chances. When someone promised they would do better, I believed them. When someone said they were working on changing themselves, I had faith that they had the tools and ability to do so. I believed in the power of transformation.

That's what I thought then. And miraculously, after all of these years, I actually do still believe that people have the power to transform themselves if they are aware, awake, and committed to that change. The thing I have learned, however, is that transformation takes a hell of a long time, and there can be a shitload of conditioning to unpack. Transformation takes place at their own pace, based on what they are willing and able to see at any given point. And there can be many setbacks. Also, not everyone is willing to go deep and do really difficult work. Sometimes it can be overwhelming to the nervous system, and they revert back to previous behavior. Again, it takes awareness to lift back out of that space.

A painful lesson that I have learned is that sometimes their unraveling can unravel you. And then there are two heaping messes. We don't always know why we stick around. And sometimes we have these arbitrary rules we set for ourselves that keep us in places that maybe we would be better off exiting. My rule since before I got divorced was, "Don't make any decisions until I am coming from a place of peace."

I didn't want to make emotional decisions because I was told as a young girl and beyond that "emotions will get you nowhere." I wasn't taught to allow my emotions to guide my decisions or choices or my view of things. I was taught to remain calm, get to a place of peace, and then dive into the data. From a place of peace, I could consider all sides. I could evaluate where the other person was coming from and if they seemed sincere. I have thought about my general rule about decision-making and reflected on what would have happened if I had made decisions from a place of emotional reactivity. What if I had not brought myself to a place of peace before taking what I thought was the next best step? Well, first of all, my life and the people in it would be very different. And further, I would have had regrets.

The societal and cultural constraints of women that were ingrained in me had a powerful influence on my decisions to give him a second chance. We learn that is our duty to sacrifice ourselves for others. We are the ones who nurture others. And somehow, a good woman can fix a man. Those limiting beliefs steered me in a very specific direction back then. I'm not so sure I would make the same choice now.

Ladies, if I knew then what I know now, I would have buckled in for the ride of my life. I know now that we are not meant to be fixers. We cannot fix other people, no matter how powerful our love is. It is up to the person who needs healing to do so for themselves. And that desire and motivation has to come from them, not us. External motivation rarely works for something so deeply ingrained. We can't fix them. Nor is it our job to do so.

Another revelation for me was that emotions *will* actually get me everywhere. It is my job to manage them and be aware of them. It is my job to feel them for myself, regardless of what anyone else says or how they feel about my emotions. I get to decide how to feel them and how to use them in my decision-making. But part of this whole human experience is to feel them and own them. Lesson learned.

CHAPTER 8

PAST-LIFE REGRESSION

I HAVE ALWAYS BEEN CURIOUS ABOUT why we are the way we are and why we have reactions to certain circumstances or events that seemingly don't make sense. Why we act the way we act, love the people we love, are fearful, and more. Additionally, I believe in past lives, and I believe in soul families. I believe that we make agreements with our soul family in previous lifetimes to join back up to fulfill promises or missions we set our hearts to. I have four children, whom I wholeheartedly believe chose me to be their mother in this lifetime. I am convinced that we had different relationships in previous lifetimes but have always been connected. I have also observed what appear to be remnants or memories of their experiences in previous lifetimes with each of my children.

For example, one evening, when my oldest daughter was ten months old, she was holding herself up in a standing position at one of our end tables. I watched her as she started making the motion of someone dipping an ink feather pen into a jar of ink and then pretending to write. I was mesmerized as she did this over and over and with great intention. She came to learn years later, through a past-life regression, that she indeed remembered this from a previous lifetime.

In June of 2014, my oldest daughter and I tossed around the idea of having a past-life regression done. We were both on spiritual journeys and wanted to dive into this other realm. A *past-life regression* is a form of hypnotherapy that takes a person back through experiences of their past lives. Even though I was curious, I had no expectations for my past-life regression. It was something I thought I would do for entertainment if nothing else. I didn't know if the person doing it was legit or not. I found her through an internet search, and she was close by. I also polled some people on social media to See if anyone else had had a past-life regression done, and one of my friends gave it a rave review. Since my daughter wanted to have one done also, we made a mommy-daughter day of it.

I remember the day. It was raining. We drove about an hour to get to the hypnotherapist's house. The hypnotherapist talked about her son, his relationship, and other random things. She had a cat that kept wanting to be next to me. I have a hard time relaxing when an animal is walking around anywhere near me because I am uncomfortable around animals. The hypnotherapist assured me the cat was fine but kept spraying the cat with a water bottle whenever she came near me. It was distracting and unnerving. But we were there, so I worked hard to calm my mind and be present. Also, we had driven an hour for this, and we had already paid our money. So, I decided to make the best of it and was able to settle in for my session as my daughter waited in the car for hers.

I decided to play along. I kept myself open to whatever might happen, but also felt some resistance to it.

Surprisingly, I walked through a few memories of lifetimes. One of them involved a severe trauma revolving around sexual assault, which did not surprise me. It took some genuine awareness and knowing what to do on the part of the hypnotherapist. She helped walk me out of there with some healing work. For that, I was grateful.

Another stop in my journey of past lives involved me being a mother of many, many children in my glory. I was sitting in a Western covered wagon, not attached to anything that could move it. There was some sort of tragedy associated with it, and it made me feel like I was a single mom. It felt like my husband had died. But there was so much joy that surrounded me with my children. It was clear that my role as a mother to many, many children was where my soul felt the fullest and most at home. These children seemed to be my reason for being. All those feelings tracked with who and how I am in this lifetime.

Equally powerful was the memory that still stands with me—a memory that may very well be one of the reasons I am still with Nick.

I was standing on top of a mountain. Not on a peak, but rather a giant rock slab. It felt like I was standing on top of the world. It was powerful and majestic. I could feel its strength and stability underneath me. I could see the glorious yellow light of the sun that shone so brightly it was almost blinding. The light took over me. For a while, it was all I could see.

And then I saw HIM. It was the silhouette of a man. A man with a cowboy hat on. He was standing there, in the light of the sun. He was a strong man, a confident man. I couldn't see his face. I could only see his form and feel his powerful energy.

An overwhelming feeling of immense, compelling, unconditional, radiant love like no other washed over me. It permeated every single cell of my body and lit my soul up. I felt my cells vibrating at a higher frequency than I have ever felt before. With every breath I took, this powerful energy grew stronger and stronger within me—through my arms and legs, my back, and into my heart. It lit my heart up and filled it so full that I felt the proverbial "my heart was overflowing." My heart felt like it was going to jump out of my chest.

When the hypnotherapist asked me to tell her what I was feeling, the only word I could utter was "love." And when she asked me if I recognized who this man was, while I could not see his face, I, very confidently, and with all the wisdom of the Universe within me and knowingness within each and every cell of my body, knew that it was Nick. He felt familiar. It was that same feeling I had when Nick and I first started talking. My familiar, comfortable home. I felt it so powerful and so undeniable that I started crying. My tears turned into sobbing, and then I couldn't stop. I had never felt or experienced a love like this in this lifetime before.

The hypnotherapist encouraged me to breathe it in and be with that feeling of love. I still remember how it felt, how the overwhelming emotions poured out of me. I remember the heat and the goosebumps and the electricity coursing through my veins.

As I look back on this experience and listen to the recordings from that session, I am reminded of the powerful force that seems to bind us together. In this lifetime and from previous lifetimes.

We are all connected. We all stem from one Source. I view us as one soul that splits off into many spirits. It is like an electric power plant. If any house contained all of the electricity that comes from a power plant, it would blow up. There are wires that run along to each house on a street, in a neighborhood, in a city, connecting each one but still separate. Likewise, we are all a part of this one soul. We are all connected by a thread. Some of us are close in proximity while others are further apart. The ones who sit close to one another have similar views and experiences and a sense of knowingness and familiarity with one another. Then there are those who sit further away from each other, and it may take longer to feel familiarity, if ever.

Years before this, when I was trying to express to Nick how I viewed us and our souls, or how I viewed people who were soul families, I used a candy necklace as an example. We are either two pieces of candy sitting next to each other, or we are on opposite sides of the strand and more distant on the soul level. I have always viewed us as two candies sitting right next to each other on that elastic thread. We know each other. We have a powerful familiarity with one another. We are meant to be together, side by side. I am guessing that Nick didn't buy into it at the time, given where we ended up. But years later, when we had our spiritual union ceremony, we exchanged rings, but also candy bracelets.

This past-life regression affirmed what I had already said out loud. We have known each other for lifetimes. He is the piece of candy right next to me on that candy necklace. How appropriate. Coach Eye Candy sitting next to me.

All of this reminds me that I have so often looked at this wounded man who stands in front of me and have felt so angry that he was placed in the various environments he was placed in during this lifetime. I know his innocence and his radiance and his purity. I see and feel his bright light. And I see the result of years and years of conditioning through his upbringing, and surrounded by others that didn't quite deserve his spirit. I see him placed in the midst of people who conditioned him to believe he wasn't enough, and being abandoned when he was fourteen years old, which ended up covering up his brilliance with countless limiting beliefs and insecurities.

Those limitations and dysfunction that came from his experiences brought him to me. For me to recognize his loving spirit and soul. And to recognize him from a previous lifetime as my love. But to also know that he has been buried deep underneath all that conditioning, so much so that he could not see or feel or remember his own radiant light. He could not access his inner light or feel his worth and divinity. But I remembered.

In later years, what made me angry was that we finally found one another in this lifetime, and the work ahead of us to truly see one another and feel the depth of love that we have felt in previous lifetimes felt insurmountable.

When I sat through my past-life regression, and after, as I reflected on it, I was certain that Nick was my cowboy. He was my love. And how blessed was I to have him back in this lifetime? How damn lucky were we that we found each other?!

In those moments during the past-life regression and as I shared my experiences with him, I was 100% certain that he was the love of all lifetimes. What I didn't know then was that I was the only one of us that truly believed in past-life regressions and that this was a "meant to be" relationship. I was the only one who believed that this was the reuniting of two souls who have known each other forever. I didn't know that because I had scientific proof, but regardless, this "knowing" was all I needed to bind us together for this lifetime. Like I said before, I am fully devoted to the man that I fancy.

CHAPTER 9

POISONED

THE FIRST FOUR YEARS OF our relationship had its ups and downs. We had growing pains, but we also had some great moments. We talked on the phone every day on his way to and from work, and we started to blend our families. We vacationed together with all our kids and had family dinners and holidays. We were there for each other when the other had an issue with a child or needed help. In 2012, when I had a gall bladder attack and a fever, Nick drove me to the hospital and was there to bring me home after my gall bladder was removed. Nick helped my oldest daughter with her science project and helped my youngest son learn how to carve a boat out of a piece of wood. When my house flooded in 2012, Nick came to the rescue and helped with a plan for my remodel. He taught my children various skills related to sanding, painting, and putting up stone over our existing brick fireplace. He redesigned my deck and enlisted my children in the reconstruction of it. He showed them how to measure, saw, and figure out angles. He was patient and kind with them as they learned. I was happy they had a male role model to teach them.

Nick and I were very active. We met most mornings at our local gym for a spinning class. I loved it so much that I became an instructor. In any given week, I taught four spinning classes and a bootcamp at a local gym and several yoga classes at the yoga studio I had opened in January of 2014. It was a dream of mine come true. Nick helped with the design work because he is so gifted at that sort of thing. My yoga and meditation studio was amazing. I felt like I was living my best life and was excited about my new business endeavor.

All of that came to a screeching halt in July of 2014, only a few short weeks after discovering that Nick was my love of all lifetimes in my past-life regression.

I took an antibiotic, called Ciprofloxacin, for a urinary tract infection. Within a week of starting it, I started noticing a twinge of elbow tendon pain. By the end of that week, the tendon pain had spread to just about every tendon in my body. I had muscle and nerve pain throughout my body. My wrists and ankles were in incredible pain. My hands cramped up just trying to use a fork to eat. I could no longer walk. I could no longer squeeze a shower scrubby. I couldn't open a gallon of milk. Showering became a chore. I crawled up the stairs each night to get myself into bed and sobbed myself to a very disjointed sleep. I slept with wrist braces on, propped up by six pillows under various body parts, just to be able to rest for a half an hour without excruciating pain. I went from teaching multiple fitness classes and kicking my own butt to being in a wheelchair overnight. One of my scariest moments was when I was adding up my continuing education credits to renew my pharmacist's license, and I could not add one plus one. My oldest daughter patiently and lovingly helped me work through the math problem.

I suffered cognitive decline. My brain did not work. I turned on the stove, and the moment I turned around, forgot what I was doing and walked away. On separate occasions, food caught on fire in the oven, and I threw a hand towel on an open flame on the stove. One night I could not remember how to turn the hot water on. I panicked and debated on whether or not I should wake my child up to help me at 1:00 a.m. on a school night. I had to stop working at a local pharmacy because I couldn't stand, and my brain didn't work. I was afraid I was going to hurt someone. As for my yoga studio, well, teaching yoga classes was impossible.

During this time, Nick came to my house almost daily to massage my arms and legs. Anything to diminish the pain. He massaged my legs and arms until I fell asleep at night, then left to go home. He did what he could to help lift my spirits. Most days, he found me curled up in a ball on a chair in the family room, doing deep breathing to help with the pain. If I was lucky, I had a five-minute reprieve from the pain.

I wanted to get out of the house one day, so I asked Nick and my oldest daughter if they would take me to the mall. I walked in between the two of them. Each of them holding me up, our arms around each other, and walking at a snail's pace. I used them to take the weight off my legs. I couldn't use crutches because my shoulders, arms, and wrists were in immense pain. Nick suggested that we rent a wheelchair so that I could enjoy some outings. At first, my pride kept me from saying yes, but eventually, I agreed. Nick tirelessly pushed me around in the wheelchair in stores, making me laugh with his silly antics. At times, I thought he was going to run me right into a display, when he would cut to the left or right at the last minute. He took me to a Pride Fest in Cleveland Downtown and pushed me around the city afterward. We had a trip to New York City planned, and I was about to cancel it when he suggested we rent a wheelchair there. He pushed me around for miles upon miles each day so I could see the sights. We laughed as we traveled through the streets. We stopped and had New York style pizza, my favorite. We rented a tandem bike and rode through Central Park. As we were passing some people on the side, one of them yelled to him, "She's not working!" because I was just sitting there on the back, not pedaling. He did all the work because I couldn't. As he continued pushing me around in the wheelchair, he leaned down repeatedly to kiss the top of my head or my cheek. He never once complained. He really showed up for me.

Before this, I didn't feel his full commitment to me. But his dedication to me in those months following the poisoning made me rethink my position on that. He showed up. Every day. This made us stronger. I felt supported and loved. I felt like nothing could break us.

Except what I didn't know then, was that he was showing up because he felt responsible for my demise. His affair had started just weeks before I got the UTI. Just before I started the anti-biotic. What I didn't know at the time was that when I texted him the terrible news that I had this debilitating side effect, he immediately thought, *this is my fault.*

Well…shit.

It took me two years, thousands of dollars, hundreds of massages, many detoxes, hours upon hours spent in an infrared sauna, a boatload of supplements, strict dietary practices, lots of tears, lots of depression and yanking myself out of it, multiple vision boards, and incredible support from my loved ones to re-cover from this. And wouldn't you know it, within weeks of me coming up for air from this ordeal, I received eight emails from his mistress.

PART 2

The Mess

Cocoon

Uncovering an affair will also uncover and unravel many parts of you. Part two of this book is about the mess that has to be worked through. This part isn't easy. For me, it was the undoing of me before I could put myself back together.

CHAPTER 10

GIVE YOURSELF GRACE

A PRIL 1 AT EXIT 22 in Tennessee was just the beginning of the cyclone that was about to hit my life. I had no idea of the depth and breadth of the dysfunction, the damage, and the details I would learn about in the coming days, weeks, and months.

This mistress had sent me very detailed emails, and my primitive brain responded with the need for more information. It wanted to figure out what was true and what was not. It was a quest for the truth because it felt like everything I had known was a lie.

You would think I had learned my lesson when my first marriage ended because of my husband's affair. I asked for so many details, thinking more information was better. I thought I needed to know it all so I could process it instead of letting my imagination take the lead and make things worse than they actually were. But alas, I didn't learn this important tidbit well enough.

Be careful what you ask for. Once you know something, you cannot unknow it. Once you see something, you cannot unsee it.

Once you hear something, you cannot unhear it. Your nervous system can go on overdrive every single time you see something that even resembles it. Or every time an image pops into your head.

Let me just tell you, my imagination could not have created some of the things I learned. And let me reaffirm to you—be careful what you ask for. Because again…once it is out, the damage has just begun. The damage continues with a dysregulated nervous system and, for me, with inadequate counselors who had no idea how to help a woman being bombarded by triggers.

I downloaded all this information swiftly because I didn't stop asking questions. I kept filing the additional information away, not wanting to fully ingest it or let it take me down.

Those first two weeks after the big reveal, I didn't even take time to curl up in fetal position in a dark room. The thought didn't even cross my mind. I was bound and determined not to let this affect my life. Some might call it shock and denial. I called it resilience. I fueled myself with my anger and carried on with my life. I didn't take the time to sit and feel sorry for myself. I thought that was what strength was. I had to show my kids that their mom could weather anything. That as their mom, I would always rise.

I had been training for my first half marathon since being crippled by an antibiotic only two years before and had just started to reclaim my life from that fiasco when the big reveal happened. But I was not going to let anything get in the way of me achieving my goal of completing this half marathon. Especially Nick's poor choices. As sad as I was about the affair, I was motivated by the vision of the triumph of completing a half marathon. This was going to be a huge exclamation point at the end of my very devastating two-year battle with fluoroquinolone toxicity. I also wanted to make my children proud. They had watched me and helped me heal through that ordeal, and I wanted to do this for them. Most importantly, I needed to prove to myself that I had indeed recovered. That I had weathered that god-awful storm, and I had come out on top.

I had to prove that I had officially reclaimed my life. That meant I needed to keep my mind strong, and I needed to make sure I took care of my body. I needed to make sure I was eating the right foods, getting a good amount of sleep, meditating, doing my visualization exercises, and moving my body—in the form of running, of course.

I continued my training, partly fueled by anger, which I am sure also helped my mindset in dealing with the affair. I had endorphins racing through my body with each run, and I felt strong. I kept myself focused on how far I had come in my physical healing and that nothing would get in the way of that.

I completed the half marathon on a very symbolic day. It was seriously one of the craziest weather days I have ever experienced. It rained, sleeted, snowed. There was lightning and thunder. Hail pelted the side of my face and body in high winds as I ran over a long bridge along Lake Erie. That part stung. The sun even peeked out, warming things up for only a moment. My race ended in a cold downpour. In the end, I finished strong, but got hypothermia soon after. I felt like I had weathered every storm during the race. I felt like Mother Nature had thrown everything my way to take a good hard look at it and decide how I wanted to proceed. And I felt like I completely rocked it. I took every bit of discomfort with a smile. Literally a smile. I had already been through hell and back with my health issues. I felt confident that I could weather any storm in my life. I knew that I had the strength, resilience, and fortitude to do so. This half marathon truly was the exclamation point at the end of that. I finished strong in my mind because of my focus, determination, and commitment to myself. Yay me!

Pushing through the initial shock of the affair would only get me so far. What I didn't realize is that I was suppressing my feelings. I was doing the dreaded spiritual bypass (when you try to avoid all the human emotions and skip to the "enlightenment" stage) that I came to loathe further down my path. Continuing along this path of suppression and anger would be okay if I wanted to let this experience make me bitter and live out the rest of my days in anger and distrust. It was fine if I was okay with not feeling love or experiencing true joy or happiness. Sure, I could carry this anger around like it was a necessary part of my existence. That's easy. But what kind of life would that be?

What I know now, in every fiber of my being, is that it is healthy to give yourself grace and hibernate for a while. It is important to honor those very hurt and damaged parts of you in the form of lying in bed, watching TV, and eating ice cream for dinner. I urge you to honor that, and I also caution you to not get stuck there, in the space of victimhood. Go fetal. You are allowed to curl up in your bed and hibernate or cry until you are done.

It is okay to ask for help to pick up the other pieces of your life while you need it. People don't know what to do or how to help. While they may not be able to mend the pieces of your shattered heart, they can certainly help with meal prep, taking your kid to soccer practice, or cleaning your house. Whatever it is, I know that we moms think we have to do it all by ourselves. That's not the case. It is okay to not have it all figured out. It is okay to let your family see your hurt and sadness, and it is okay to let them help soothe your pain.

It is okay to say no to the betrayer when he thinks he wants to talk to ease his conscience. It is utterly okay to place his needs last on your list, or even throw them away so they're not even in front of you or in your awareness. It is not your job to make him feel better about what he did. It is okay to prioritize yourself despite what social and cultural conditioning tells us as women. It is not our job to fix the dysfunctional man standing in front of us. That is his damn job.

Not only is it okay or healthy, but it is absolutely necessary to honor yourself and nurture yourself in times of great trauma. There is a little girl within me, my inner child, who probably needed some protection from all that was happening. She knows now that I will always have her back. It took me far too long to realize this one.

This is just the tip of the iceberg to the transformation process that the big reveal started. This next section of the book is going to go into some places that were really tough for me. This is where the proverbial seed cracked open, and it looked like it was the end of my world. But it turned out to be the beginning of tremendous growth and transformation.

This next section picked me up several times, shook me up, and spit me back out, leaving me to somehow try to reorient myself. There were, what felt like infinite moving pieces and various dynamics, setbacks, and successes, and then more setbacks that I had to work through to get to where I am now, which is a damn good place.

Key Takeaways

1. Take the time to go fetal. Cry it out. As often as you need to. You'll know when you're ready to rise.

2. Honor your feelings and allow yourself time to nurture yourself with comfort foods and plenty of rest. Hibernate if you need to.
3. Give yourself grace. Unapologetically say no to things you don't feel like doing.
4. Remember that you are responsible for you, and you alone.
5. Let the people who want to help you help you.

CHAPTER 11

WHY?

ONE OF THE BIG QUESTIONS I asked myself (and him), when I learned about the affair, was *WHY?*

In April 2016, I was working as a pharmacist part-time. I had an amazing coworker, Susanne, who also happened to be my very close friend. Over the time I worked there, we talked about all sorts of topics: cooking and recipes, even relationships. When I returned to work after our vacation, Susanne cried when I told her about the big reveal.

In the weeks and months that followed, Susanne and I spent countless hours talking about affairs and why they happen. We talked about the porn industry and how the internet makes pornography accessible at the tip of a finger. The porn industry promotes unrealistic and harmful expectations of what it is to be a man, what it is to be a woman, and what is reasonable to expect in the bedroom. It creates a false sense of what sexuality is, what turns people on, and what true intimacy is.

We considered the messages society sends to men. We talked about what it means to be a "man," and the stigma that is placed upon a man who is sensitive and caring versus one who is a "man's man." We talked about Tiger Woods and the other men who have claimed to have sex addictions and how that has played out for them. We talked about the men who cheat on their gorgeous wives with stunning bodies. And we discussed how a man's upbringing can leave him feeling like he is not enough to the point where he will try anything to show his worth and build himself up. We talked about using sex to numb pain that is buried deep, and how people in general thrive off dopamine hits to their brains. And sex, secrecy, and "getting away with something" can give those bursts of dopamine, making the person feel a high.

We also talked about how people thoughtlessly cast the blame on the woman. They say that if there wasn't something wrong in the house, the man wouldn't stray. I considered this. But while we explored all of the potential reasons, the answer to WHY, in my situation, felt unanswered.

In my earliest conversations with Nick after the big reveal, I asked a lot of very pointed questions. I thought that somehow my brain could pinpoint exactly WHY this happened. I thought his answers would provide an a-ha moment when everything suddenly made sense.

During those initial days, I knew inside myself that this affair had nothing to do with me. I had experience with this, after all. When my first marriage ended with an affair, I spent a great deal of time reading books written by famous people about their experiences with affairs. Many of these women were successful, drop-dead gorgeous, empowered women with perfect bodies. Clearly, their men had problems.

It took me a while to learn that my ex-husband's affairs had nothing to do with me. That it was not a call to action for me to change anything about who I was. So, my first reaction to this most recent big reveal was that it had nothing to do with me. I was just angry.

Out of control angry. Two middle fingers an inch from his face, yelling "Fuck you" angry. But eventually I realized that this emotional reaction was not getting me anywhere good.

I don't think there is anyone who has gone through a betrayal who doesn't search for the answer to the big question, "Why?"

It is as if knowing the answer to that question will somehow flip the magical switch in the brain that allows us to comprehend the atrocity of a blatant betrayal. In doing so, it would theoretically help us release the anger, access the peace we so desperately want, and move on with our lives. It seems like knowing the answer to the question "Why?" would give us closure.

In our quest for this answer, our minds can take us to some dark places.

We look to the other woman. *What does she have that I don't have? What was so special about her?* The comparisons continue. *What is wrong with me? Is my butt too big? Are my boobs too small? Are my lips not plump enough? Do I not perform well?* Then we beg. *Someone just give me an answer to this so I can get on with my life!*

For me, as I examined the answers to these superficial questions, I laughed. It wasn't that. There was literally no comparison between me and her.

A defining moment

I used my anger to fuel me and keep me on my feet as I continued my quest for the answer to *WHY*.

All of that came to a screeching halt less than two months later, when I gave myself a concussion. I will talk more about it in another chapter. But essentially, in a heated moment of frustration, I hit myself on the head repeatedly with the palms of my hands, trying to get the deep emotional pain to stop. I begged the Universe to make it all go away. That was a defining moment of how I would navigate the next year, at least. This is when all of the self-doubts, anxiety, depression, and triggers became completely unmanageable. I had no ability to self-regulate. I lost my strength and resilience.

This is when my journey to becoming a shell of my former self began.

I continued asking WHY more desperately. *Why did he do this? Why did he risk losing the best thing he ever had? Why did he make up all of those stories in his head about me, which were completely wrong? Why her? What did she have to offer that I didn't? How could he do this? How could he look me in the face and tell me he loved me and then turn around and do something like this? How could he be living two lives? And how could he, for a moment, live with himself?*

Then I turned on myself. *What in the hell is wrong with me? Why do I attract men who are unfaithful? What about me is not enough? Am I enough? Why am I not enough? Why is it impossible for a man to love me fully for who I am? Will I be abandoned again? And then what does my life look like? Why am I being rejected— AGAIN? What is even loveable about me? When he says he loves me, WHY does he say that?*

My anxious brain kept searching for answers that made sense. It wanted to be reassured that I was loved, and I was enough. But a part of my brain would not let logical and reasonable answers in. The part of me that was filled with self-doubt was lit up like a raging fire, and something in me was holding me down, not allowing me to rise from that. This was new to me. I was literally turning on myself. And this was the start of my self-abandonment.

What I thought then was that if someone told me WHY, then it would rationally make sense, and the self-doubting and self-loathing would miraculously go away. If I knew the reason WHY my whole life had to turn upside down, then I could magically become whole again, take the lessons, and be a better person. And the sooner someone could tell me exactly WHY, the sooner I could resume my life, open my heart, feel love, laughter, and joy, and sail off into the sunset. It would put an end to my suffering. Instantaneously.

Right? Isn't this why we think we want to know why? In our quest for the answer to this very big question, we ask and ask for details so our brains can try to wrap themselves around this horrible trauma. And we learn facts that we actually didn't want to know. We learn specifics that make it worse. Our suffering increases. And then the triggers increase because now we have even more information to feed our overactive imaginations.

What I know now is that there is no reasonable answer to the question of WHY. There is no answer that will ever be acceptable and make the pain and hurt go away. There is nothing anyone could say to me that would be met with the response, "Oh, okay! That makes sense. Phew! Good to know. Now everything is better."

I looked at myself for about a minute. But I knew it had nothing to do with me. I know other women who look to themselves and think they caused their partner to have an affair. They feel like if they are the reason for the affair, then at least they can control something about it. They can change and morph into someone their partner says he wants. They can try to "win" their cheating spouse back. I caution women against this. No one forced their partner to have sex with someone else. That is on them and them alone.

I could have speculated why Nick cheated. He was selfish. He made bad decisions. His need for a dopamine hit outweighed his sense of reasoning and good moral choices. That same dopamine hit overrode his sense of integrity, his good conscience, and commitment to me. That dopamine rush was worth the devastation and destruction that would impact not just my life, but our whole ecosystem as we would work for years to rebuild. The scientific reason for things appeals to me. I can start to wrap my head around the tangible aspects of scientific evidence. But that just circles around to him being *selfish*, which Merriam-Webster dictionary defines as "concerned excessively or exclusively with oneself/ seeking or concentrating on one's own advantage, pleasure, or well-being without regard for others." Yep, this fit the bill.

Alternatively, let's pretend that the "why" had anything to do with the other woman. Let's, for the sake of fiction, say she was prettier, had bigger boobs, was more adventurous. Let's say she was intellectually stimulating, had a great personality, made him laugh incessantly, and was irresistible. In either scenario, is there anything in those words that brings a sense of closure or understanding? Or peace? Hell no, not for me.

The reality of the entire fictional assessment of the other woman is the opposite. There was nothing that overtly special about her. But even when I learned negative things about her, it did not bring me satisfaction or a sense of relief. It created more questions. *Why in the hell was he attracted to someone he didn't even respect?* It didn't make rational sense to me. In a world where women are pitted against one another, some find it enough to learn terrible truths about the other woman. It feels like it is enough to have their man trash talk the mistress. I will admit, it did give me some pleasure. But the underlying question remained. If she is so unappealing, then WHY?

Early on, Nick answered the question "WHY" many, many times: "Because I am an asshole, and I had my head up my ass." Nothing else, at the time, made sense. But this one started to. Months and years later, he would admit that he was full of anger for the world. And that anger informed the choices he made.

But before he made that revelation, some things just needed to be surrendered to the Universe. And one of those was the actual answer to all of these questions. This did not happen overnight. It took years for me to surrender some of it, on my own timeline. The greatest transformations happen when we surrender. I surrendered my need to understand WHY from a rational place in my mind.

More important than knowing his reason for WHY was that I needed to know, without a shadow of a doubt, that it truly had nothing to do with me. It had nothing to do with my inner or outer beauty, who I am as a loving, kind person, a terrific mother and phenomenal, supportive friend. It had nothing to do with the frequency of sex I was comfortable with. It had nothing to do with the fact that I am compassionate, naive at times, fun-loving, and light-hearted. It had nothing to do with the level of mama bear that comes out whenever one of my loved ones has been wronged. It had nothing to do with the fact that I love watching romantic comedies, or cooking, or organizing a whole family get-together. It had nothing to do with my love of baking more than anyone will eat. It had nothing to do with my connectedness to the Universe or my devotion to my spirituality. It had nothing to do with the fact that I prefer deep conversation and connection over shallow interactions. It had nothing to do with me being an introvert and enjoying hibernation time alone. Or that I am not a morning person and don't want anyone even looking in my direction until well after noon. It had nothing to do with me having adverse reactions to the sounds of other people chewing. Or my lack of patience in lines, in places packed with people, and maybe just lack of patience in general. It had nothing to do with the fact that I have shoes lying around at each door or have organized (and disorganized) piles of papers on my desk. It had nothing to do with my graying hair, my aging body, my wrinkles around my eyes.

It had nothing to do with me. Period.

What I have come to know about the whole ordeal is that hurt people hurt people. And hurt people are prone to self-sabotage. Everyone has dark and light within them. And everyone has the ability to choose what they choose to express and put energy into. We all come with our conditioning, our baggage, our idea of what love looks like, and our idea of what it feels like to belong.

When people grow up in homes that lack positive reinforcement and are filled with yelling voices, they have no real idea what love and respect look like. They end up fighting for themselves and have a hard time believing that anyone could actually love them for them. It is impossible for them to fully trust another human being to have their back. They don't feel like they are enough. They have fought hard to survive and look only to themselves, relying on nobody outside of themselves. So, when someone like me comes along, it is the scariest thing in the world. No one can possibly be this pure of heart. No, not in their world. And even if they remotely think that they have someone good in their life, they self-sabotage before the person leaves so they don't put themselves at risk of abandonment. They see the world through dirt-covered glasses. And they make choices that reinforce their conditioned worldview. Until something changes, until their world is entirely rocked, until there is an actual shift, they continue to make poor choices.

It's not that he didn't think I was enough. It was that he didn't think HE was enough.

Key Takeaways

1. His affair is not your call to action to change.
2. His affair was not your fault. He made the choice, and it had nothing to do with you.
3. Hurt people hurt people.

CHAPTER 12

HEALING—THE TICKING CLOCK

T HE PAIN OF THIS BETRAYAL was unbearable, and the hope of better days kept me going. I had been through enough other tough situations in life to know that everything passes. *But how long would it be before I would be able to go through an entire day without thinking about it or feeling it? How long does it take to heal from a betrayal of trust?*

One thing that I told myself back then was that within two years, we should be back to normal. I had read somewhere about an algorithm based on the number of years someone had been together. I hung my hat on their prediction of two years. But when I reached the two-year mark, I felt frustrated and borderline hopeless. I looked at the triggers I was still having and kept asking when they would end. I was still having difficulty moving through them at times, and when they arose, it felt like my whole world stopped.

But as the saying goes, if it doesn't feel good yet, you are still in the middle. Keep going.

That arbitrary number of years that it should take to move through the grief and heal—written by some clinical psychologist—is a bunch of bullshit. There is *no* timeline. Everyone is different, and the only timeline that matters is your own, naturally evolving timeline. It's okay to keep it open ended! There is already so much failure and fear and feelings of not being enough or good enough surrounding an affair. The threat of a failed timeline can make you feel like you're swimming in a whole ocean of failure.

It is not up to anyone else to determine how long you get to grieve or process things. An affair is not just that someone had sex with someone else. There are layers and layers of shit that get piled on to every bit of insecurity you ever had even prior to this relationship. Those insecurities get lit up like a raging fire. And it is a lot to handle.

Years later, I know that I could have given myself much more grace and not listened to the people outside of me who said it was time to let it go. There were a lot of mini choices along the way. One foot in and one foot out, trusting versus not trusting. Trusting all but five percent, and so on and so forth. Each mini choice led me to the next best choice, and whether it led to conflict, a flood of emotions, or a triumph, each and every one of those choices led me to where I am now.

Healing is not linear. It is a path of jagged peaks and troughs along the way, trending upward toward wholeness. Rather than assessing healing daily, I started comparing my progress with where I was a month prior to that moment. Keeping that in mind as a more realistic healing path can help circumvent those low moments of hopelessness. There were many times I felt like giving up, throwing in the towel, and burning the whole relationship to the ground. In those moments of deep pain and frustration, and anger—so much anger, trying to protect my heart—it all seemed hopeless. It's normal. No relationship is all puppies and daisies. There will be conflict.

What I learned during the bouts of conflict that surrounded the affair, the healing path, and the spiritual expansion that was happening was this: You are not your reaction. You are not that initial trigger reaction. You are not defined by how you react based on years of conditioning and the unprocessed baggage you carry. You are how you respond after that initial reaction. What that means is that maybe the first reaction is to defend or attack in a moment of a trigger or frustration to that trigger. But what happens in the next few moments matters more. It is how you choose to proceed after you realize you are having an instinctual reaction. It is what happens once you step outside of the primitive, fight-or-flight part of your brain and inside your thinking brain. There is a moment, if you can step into your awareness, that you get to pause and breathe and choose a different action that is more indicative of where you are on your healing path and your commitment to change and transform. That is what matters.

It took me a while to figure that piece out. In most cases, I stuck by my initial reaction, afraid to surrender it. I was afraid that if I did, somehow the emotion I was fighting so hard for would be invalidated. My need to be heard and my right to express my feelings outweighed my ability to see that I was slowly turning into someone who, if I continued down this path, would never trust the world again.

Additionally, my need to protect myself made me think that Nick's initial reactions were who he was deep down inside. In the beginning, when I had triggers that sent my nervous system reeling, Nick's first reaction was defensiveness. From his place of guilt and shame, he had a hard time acknowledging and validating my triggers, which only made matters worse. He didn't know what defensiveness looked like until he modeled it for one of the counselors we saw, who quickly pointed it out. I viewed his defensiveness as complete and utter dismissal of my intense feelings. Nick learned and evolved, and his initial reactions became less and less defensive. He was generally able to take a breath. However, there were rare instances when he fell back into that initial defensive reaction. It was then that I didn't allow myself to recognize that literally only a moment later, he had already returned to his thinking brain. And from his thinking brain, he was validating, loving, and compassionate. This was the part of him that wanted to repair the damage that he had done. This was him showing up from having done a TON of work on himself.

But I was stuck in my primitive, self-protective brain. He could throw all the love in the world at me, but I was stuck in my old definition of myself. The self that wasn't allowed to use her voice but was fighting to burst through that barrier. Further, I was stuck in my assessment of him being who he was, with the sole criterion being his initial, instinctive reaction. So, I didn't let it in. I could not hear the goodness in his heart or allow his love into mine. This, my friends, made my healing timeline so much longer. I stood in my own way of getting to what I wanted.

Years later, through many ups and downs, I recognized that Nick had been standing in his truth and honor all this time. He had been on a learning curve for sure. It didn't happen overnight. But he had been showing up consistently, and I had been pushing hard against him. I had to be sure that whatever he was bringing would stand the test of time. Since I have a fierce desire to protect myself, my walls did not come down easily.

I don't beat myself up over it because it is during those times of me pushing him away that I eventually found myself for myself. It was during those dark moments, when I felt the emptiness within, that I turned to myself and started doing the deeper healing I needed to do. Healing childhood wounds, feminine and masculine wounds, reflecting on the conditioning and limiting beliefs about myself affected my perceptions and all my relationships—not just my relationship with Nick. A lot of my wounds didn't come from just this affair. When I stood in the darkness, the cracks from my wounds allowed light to come shining in and heal places in me that needed to be healed.

The catalyst sucked. And a lot of the process sucked. But where I am today, I would never have been if it weren't for those individual moments —those very tumultuous moments—and each mini choice.

Coming back to my initial question: How long does it take to heal?

Everyone's timeline is different. There is no shame in taking your time and wanting deeper, spiritual healing and making sure you get there. The timeline is not for someone outside of you to choose. It is not when someone tells you to let it go or get over it. It is not when the sand in the hourglass has passed to the bottom. There is no ticking clock. It is your timeline and yours alone.

I know now that it is ever evolving and will probably be with me for the rest of my life. But the triggers diminish. It's not as large of a part of my life as it was in the beginning. And when things come up, I don't have to beat myself for feeling anxious about a trigger for something that happened in the past. It is what it is. It happened. I don't have to look at myself as a failure for having a thought about it, or being triggered years later by something that comes up. Because I am not a failure. I knew that in choosing to stay with him, this would be part of the fabric of our relationship. There is always healing to be done. I am a human being with very human emotions. And so are you. The healing continues.

Honor your timeline.

Key Takeaways

1. There is no timeline except the one that is right for you.
2. Try measuring where you are compared to where you were a month before. It can help figure out a more realistic healing path. Healing is not linear. It is a jagged path that trends upward.
3. You are not your reaction. What you choose (how you respond) after the initial reaction is more indicative of where you are on your healing path.

CHAPTER 13

CONCUSSION

I THOUGHT I WAS DOING PRETTY well for the first few months after the big reveal. I was focused on my training for the half marathon. I had endorphins racing through my veins. I slept well, meditated every day, went to the local park and looked over the lake most days. I took picnic lunches with me, set out a blanket, read a book, and took in the beauty of nature. I was grounding myself. I connected to all my self-care practices, expressed myself coherently, and was able to function very well during those last few months of the school year and into the summer.

But one night in July, some fierce triggers came to a head. I had visions of what might have happened during the affair. I saw him. I saw her. I felt deeply rejected and betrayed. I was swimming in a sea of trigger reactions and found myself completely overwhelmed. I was in a fit of anger, rage, and sadness.

We had a conversation, and I wanted my feelings to be heard. I wanted validation. But in those moments, Nick was stuck in his defensiveness. Big time. No matter what I described, his response was a statement of all the work he was doing to better himself. I didn't want to hear about all the work he was doing. I wanted to be validated. I wanted him to understand my experience. The more I spoke, the more anger and fury seeped out of me. With each defensive statement he made, I fought for my right to speak and feel. At some point along the way—I suspect early in our conversation—he reverted to identifying with his guilt and shame triggers. When he was in that space, all he could do was defend himself. And for me, this was the absolute last thing I needed or wanted from him.

In that fit of complete and utter frustration with him and disconnection from myself, I hit myself on the head with the palms of my hands.

Repeatedly.

I sobbed and asked the Universe to erase the whole experience from my head. Not just the experience of the big reveal, but my whole experience with him, from the moment we even set eyes on one another until now. I wanted it all to be gone. Like our relationship never happened. I wanted everything to be erased from my memory and for me to go back to a time of innocence. A time before Nick.

Nick didn't know what to do. He left my house in a hurry, leaving me in a ball of tears.

The next morning, I woke to go to work. I was operating on four hours of sleep and a lot of tears. So, I expected a headache. My head pounded at work under the fluorescent lights and staring at the computer. My eyes hurt. Every sound made me want to cover my head and hide.

The day after that, I still had an intense headache. Lights and sounds still made my head pound. The only thing that made me feel better was lying in a dark room with my eyes closed. And then the lightbulb in my head went off.

I suspected that I had given myself a concussion.

After two weeks of having this intense headache, I went to the doctor. My anxiety was through the roof. Lights and sounds still made me want to hide. I was having a hard time functioning in my daily life. I told my doctor, "I can't do life," and broke down in tears. This was a big deal. I had never cried in front of my doctor before. Not even through the antibiotic poisoning ordeal. My doctor confirmed a concussion based on my symptoms and what had led to it. But I knew what I had done two days in.

Giving myself a concussion was not one of my proudest moments. In fact, it was a moment in time that I am embarrassed of and will never forget.

It was a moment when I chose (not consciously) self-harm. I let my emotional reaction get so out of control that I actually hurt myself in a profound way. It changed the course of how I would navigate this life experience and many other difficult challenges in the coming years.

But it was also a moment in time that I would work to keep in my awareness from that point forward. Another defining moment.

For the next eleven months, I suffered with post-concussion syndrome. It impacted how I functioned every day. My head burned incessantly. I couldn't drive after dark because the lights from oncoming cars or traffic lights were too painful. I was hypersensitive to sights and sounds. I had to give up my cushy job because I couldn't function underneath the fluorescent lights and looking at the computer screen. It was excruciating.

I couldn't think clearly in conversations. I couldn't work out because any exercise that increased my heart rate and would have made me feel better by increasing my endorphins (feel-good hormones) made my head burn like crazy. When I lost my ability to work out, I lost my biggest coping mechanism. I was left to handle my triggers, my life, my relationship, my healing from a place of severe deficit. My neurotransmitters were all over the place. (*Neurotransmitters* are things like serotonin, dopamine, and norepinephrine, which help regulate your mood.) I became a frail version of myself. Any intense emotions would set off the intense burning inside my head. The pain was unbearable.

My biggest regret in this is that I couldn't function as a mom in the way I wanted to. My oldest son was leaving for college in the fall, and this was my last summer of having him home and having his friends around. This was a summer when my house was completely full of awesome kids, and I missed out on making some precious and joyful memories. I missed out on graduation parties, on spontaneous runs to the ice cream stand, and on the local town events. I missed out on the experience of joy with my kids. I missed out on family dinners most nights because I was too exhausted to cook. I hurt myself in more ways than one on that fateful night.

It ultimately led me to a point where I could not handle the depression and extreme anxiety that resulted from the imbalance of neurotransmitters in my brain and the inflammation I created. I would get anxious sitting in a room for five minutes with other people. I would get anxious looking at my calendar and seeing a massage scheduled. Really? The most relaxing thing I could imagine would illicit crippling anxiety. I stopped going out with friends. I stopped having coffee dates, even with the friends who filled me up.

I started having suicidal ideations. Every day on my way to work, I had to cross a busy intersection. I envisioned a Mack Truck hitting me every single day to take me out of the misery that was a huge part of my life. Every day was a chore. I didn't want to get out of bed in the morning and counted the hours until I could return to bed in the evening. The only thing keeping me afloat was my four kids, who needed me, even if I wasn't' the most present mom in the world. Thank God for them. They have no idea how many times they have saved me.

During this time, Nick also showed up. Each day, he took me for a walk around the block. And he showed up in the softest version of himself that he could. We talked through issues in a much calmer and regulated way. He stepped up, offering more love and compassion. He was more understanding and thoughtful of my emotional and physical health.

Eventually, I reached a pivotal point. One day I was so down that my oldest daughter, who was nineteen years old, walked to my bedroom and watched me as I slept. She was concerned about me and my mental health and wanted to make sure I was okay. This is when I realized I had to change something. This was not the life I wanted for my little girl. She had better things to do—live her life, spread her wings. To this day, I have deep regret and sorrow that my baby girl shouldered so much of my pain.

That's the day I made the conscious decision to ask for help from my doctor and start taking an antidepressant. I did not make this decision lightly. Having been crippled from the antibiotic just two years before this, I was scared out of my mind to take any medications. Liz and I hashed out many options for lifting me from the darkness. I grappled and lamented about using an antidepressant. Ultimately, it came down to needing to lift myself up, to reset my neurotransmitters, and be the mom I wanted and needed to be. I chose the antidepressant. Asking for this was the result of great desperation to somehow feel better, enough to start reclaiming my life. It was also a sign of hope. Because I could envision feeling better from this, and this was my next best step in moving in that direction. Me wanting better for my baby girl was my motivating force for me to pick myself up and do something.

We do things to ourselves when we are hurting because we want to be out of our misery. It is a moment of desperation. It is a moment of not thinking clearly. This was another defining moment (oh so many) that made me realize I was having severe mental health issues (as to be expected), and I needed help.

I realized that I harmed myself because of something outside of myself. Something was happening that I could not control. Another human being was saying things and reacting to his wounds, and I somehow allowed my nervous system to react in a BIG way, ultimately hurting myself for a long time to come. The suffering that I endured because of my own actions and inability to step away from intense conversations only hurt me. And my kids.

I knew all the positive things I could have been connecting to. I have coached clients through triggers and traumatic events. I knew how to breathe. I knew how to meditate. I knew how to surrender. But in those moments leading up to the self-harm, I did not connect to anything that made sense to me. I abandoned my self-care practices, and I abandoned myself.

My self-inflicted concussion prolonged the time it took for me to heal. It disrupted my entire system, and my healing path came to a screeching halt. It affected how my brain made and metabolized neurotransmitters, my physiology, my ability to process and cope with daily life, and especially my ability to digest the intense emotions that I was dealing with. This is perhaps my biggest regret. In a moment where I completely disconnected from all of my self-care practices, a moment of complete desperation to erase the memory of all that had happened because it was so painful—this act of self-harm set me back in many ways.

I was embarrassed, I betrayed myself, I committed an act of hate against myself, and I allowed my emotions to get the best of me in a very detrimental way. I was the only one who suffered.

My concussion was a wakeup call for both me and Nick, when we both realized how harmful and unhealthy our patterns of communication were. We both de-escalated. Sure, part of this was because I couldn't tolerate loud noises. But it was also because we both wanted to heal.

This was one of those big events that made me realize that no one, and I mean no one, is worth self-harm. In subsequent moments of frustration, I kept this realization and my huge mistake at the forefront of my mind. Never again would I even think (or not think) of hurting myself. What I didn't know then was that this was the start of my journey to getting to know the divine woman that I am and ultimately healing inner child wounds that I had carried for much of my life.

It sounds rosy from here on out. Words like *journey* and *divine* make it sound so magical. But this was anything but magical. This journey of accessing and truly embracing my divine feminine would take years of unraveling at times, and then picking myself up.

Key Takeaways

1. If you are having thoughts of self-harm or suicidal ideations, please seek the help of a healthcare professional. There is help. Ask for it. You are not alone.
2. No one is worth you harming yourself.
3. Figure out your "why." Why is it that you get up every day? Who are you living for? Keep your focus on your "why" and keep putting one foot in front of the other.

Chapter 14

Triggers

I T WASN'T UNTIL AFTER THE concussion that triggers became a huge problem for me. This is when I started turning on myself. I had a great deal of trouble regulating myself, my thoughts, my mood. A concussion, by virtue of being a mild traumatic brain injury, is essentially an assault on the central nervous system. And my nervous system was already on the edge.

To be clear, a *trigger* is a stimulus that causes a painful memory to resurface. In that memory, your body can react as if it was experiencing the memory for the first time, in real time. The pain is real. The reaction is real. The devastating agony is real. In that moment, the nervous system thinks it is happening. Right. Now.

I was haunted by triggers. They came in all forms. They included music that alluded to love, sex, secrecy, relationships, break ups—anything. I could only listen to instrumentals, which initially really sucked because I was training for a half marathon, and it was hard to find motivating and inspiring music in the form of instrumentals only. I was triggered by movies with a love interest, an affair, a sex scene, basic female/male attraction to one another, people kissing in a car, or nudity. I basically couldn't watch movies because let's face it: in movies, sex sells. It is crazy how many individual words became triggers for me. Words and phrases. Certain clothing. Anyone who had plastic surgery, or a boob job, Botox, or lip enhancement gone bad. Cars. The make and model of her car seemed to surround me wherever I went. Her apartment on the hill across the street from where I used to work out. To protect my nerves, I stopped working out there. Any form of intimacy. Kissing. I simply couldn't do it anymore. Certain phrases that were used in the days surrounding the big reveal, dates, and anniversaries that I knew about. Facebook memories with pictures during the timeframe of the affair made it all feel like one big lie. A certain look from him or a perceived emotional distance from him would send me into a tailspin. Sex was a trigger. A big one. My own body was a trigger.

I started to hate my own body. I looked at it with complete and utter disdain. Why? Because "she" was a woman, and I had something in common with her. I didn't want anything in common with her. I absolutely abhorred her and her existence. It was a massive trigger. I couldn't separate my feminine body from the thought of hers. I hated myself. I could not look at myself in the mirror. After a shower, I would run to put my clothes on.

It was a nightmare. I understand how the mind can go to some dark places. But to hate my body, my temple that houses my soul, was a new one.

But the biggest trigger, by far, was HIM. His existence.

I felt like I was swimming through triggers all by myself with no help for relief in sight. It was like being in the middle of the ocean, and one wave after another comes crashing in. One wave was somewhat manageable. But they came in at a fast pace, one on top of another, and I didn't have time to catch my breath in between the waves. I felt like I was drowning. And the more

I resisted or fought them, the more they came. It felt like the affair, visions of the affair, and details of the affair would always be right there smacking me upside the face. That they would never go away. Talk about feeling hopeless. I thought I would be stuck in this place of fear and anxiety forever.

My inability to effectively manage my triggers was a major hindrance to my healing.

I still wasn't able to step up for myself. I wanted Nick to do all the work needed to soothe my nervous system and take the pain away. Additionally, I was continuously riddled with disappointment when he wasn't able to single-handedly mend my heart.

I wished Nick would wave a magic wand to make the whole affair go away, as if it never actually happened, to make it so that the memories of all that had transpired vanished. Like they were made up. When I woke up every morning and realized it had, in fact happened, I felt deflated. When Nick couldn't magically fix everything, I got upset. Very upset. I wanted him to fix what he had broken. I wanted HIM to handle my triggers with the loving care that I couldn't give myself. I wanted a knight in shining armor to come in and fix everything for me. And I wanted that knight to be Nick. I would later accept that I, alone, was responsible for my healing and that Nick did not possess a magic wand to take my pain away.

At the time, I could not find a single resource that made me feel like I was a normal human being having a very normal experience after this trauma. I needed to have my experience validated but didn't know how to articulate that at the time. It felt like the trauma kept getting thrown into my face everywhere I turned. And I did not have the tools and resources to learn how to handle them in a healthy way.

Sure, I bought all the books AGAIN about how to heal from an affair, anger, forgiveness, trust, and anything else I could find. But none of them felt like they validated the experience I was having. My experience seemed to be off the rails inside of me. As the weeks, months, and years passed, I felt embarrassed to still be having triggers that would stop me in my tracks. *Why wasn't I over this yet? And why was there this invisible timeline when I was no longer allowed to be triggered or have an intense reaction to something that brought it all back to me?* Eventually I stopped talking about the impact of my triggers to my closest friends because I thought that they felt it was time for me to move on. But I had not yet reached that point in my healing. I needed more. I needed to feel safe within myself. And I wasn't there yet.

From Nick's perspective, in the heat of my triggers, I was *choosing* to go back in time and feel this. But for me, it was the most devastating thing about most of my days. *Why on earth would I ever CHOOSE this?* I could be having a perfectly great day, and then suddenly, the wind would blow in a certain direction, and thoughts and visions flooded back into my head. Or we could be having a relaxing night together watching a movie, and then a vivid sex scene would trigger me and send me reeling.

Whenever I was triggered and unable to settle my mind, I felt like all of my hard work, blood, sweat, and tears were invalidated in Nick's mind because I was having a tough moment. It sucked to be in this state of disarray. It was difficult to "snap" out of it, even when I knew it was a trigger, and I wasn't experiencing the "real event" in the moment. The jolt of stress hormones and the disruption to my day threw me for a loop and left me gasping for air. And I was the kind of person who didn't just bounce back after each event. My system would be completely spent after each episode. It would take me at least an overnight sleep to calm myself and be able to breathe again.

I have said it before, and I will say it again. The arbitrary timeline of when this should all pass, and life should return to normal is utter bullshit. There is no timeline. Everyone heals at their own rate and to their own level of satisfaction. A betrayal can certainly create wounds, but it can also cut old wounds wide open. It can bring awareness to wounds that felt like they were scarred over, and it can rip those scabs right off, exposing every other unhealed layer beneath them. Some people move through their grief quickly. Others don't. It's okay. What doesn't help is the expectations from people outside of the relationship and the misplaced judgment of how others think you should be progressing.

I wanted nothing more than for all the triggers to completely go away. But they came at any damn time they wanted. When triggers came, I raged. Anger surged out from every pore of my body. And even when I probably should have tapped out of an argument, I kept going. I could not self-regulate.

One piece of advice I received from a counselor later in the journey was that when I become aware that I am in a dysregulated state, I should then make a conscious decision to pause. Take a break, breathe, set aside a certain amount of time to collect myself and ground myself. Then come back to the conversation from a more regulated place.

It sounds simple, I know. But whenever I was in that state of fight or flight, I was NOT in my thinking brain. This didn't help matters. First of all, he couldn't understand what I was trying to explain about my needs or my triggers. As soon as I rose my voice, his defenses went up, and nothing further reached his brain. Naturally my voice rose when I was having an intense mental and physical reaction because I did not feel safe. And second, if the goal was to work through things and work toward a stronger relationship, then this method of me raging with each trigger was clearly not working.

Each argument created one more thing to pile on the list of things to heal from. As if the list wasn't long enough. I didn't know this. I wasn't educated about how this might play out. I was lost. It took a while for me to eventually realize that the triggers would not completely go away. And my reaction to them and how I navigated them would be more instrumental not only in my healing, but in the healing of our relationship.

Believe me, I worked on regulating my nervous system. When passing by certain places, my nervous system would just wig out. I learned to predict when this would happen and would start repeating to myself over and over, "I am safe. I am safe. I am safe." I had to train my brain to know I was safe, taming that primitive part of the brain that senses danger.

There is a Buddhist teaching that encourages people to lean into pain. Feel it. Face it. I had learned this concept earlier in my life, and historically would lean into painful situations instead of boxing them out or walling them off. When the big reveal happened, I thought I was supposed to lean into the pain in order to process and move through it. So, I leaned in. And I leaned in some more. And I kept leaning into every single little thing that came my way. I didn't know that by leaning in over and over, I would end up overwhelming my nervous system and feel even more frazzled.

I had fully trained my brain to react intensely to triggers. And by continuously exposing myself to them by leaning in, my brain was wired to be hypervigilant, treat everything as a threat, and to react. I felt it in every cell of my body. I felt depressed and anxious. I couldn't feel joy. I felt tired. I was exhausted. I slept poorly and woke up groggy. I couldn't motivate myself for simple pleasures. Leaning in all the time was not the way to go. I was completely overwhelmed. I was in a constant state of fight or flight. By having a chronically dysregulated nervous system, it ultimately manifested as a host of physical health problems.

* * *

The bottom line is to *pace yourself with the triggers*. There is no need to be a hero or a martyr. The only one who gets harmed is you. It is okay to pick and choose what to lean into and what to ignore at any given moment. For me, going out of my way to avoid triggers so I was exposed to them at a slow to moderate level was a better way to go. It allowed my nervous system a chance to rest.

This didn't come easy though. Read on for your ninety-second science lesson for today.

The *sympathetic nervous system* is the part of the nervous system that is responsible for the fight-or-flight reaction. It is what produces the feelings of anxiety and fear. When the nervous system becomes dysregulated, the sympathetic nervous system is basically dominant. It is in overdrive.

The *parasympathetic nervous system* is the part of the nervous system that calms and soothes the mind and body. It involves the vagus nerve, which runs through most parts of your body. This is how the brain communicates with your organs. This is what tells your heart rate to slow down and your blood pressure to regulate. This is the part of the nervous system that needs to be activated to quiet the dominant sympathetic nervous system.

But how?

The quickest way to change the state of your mind and body is through breath. What do we do when we are stressed or in fight or flight? We stop breathing. We hold our breath. In doing so, we withhold precious life force from entering our bodies.

My advice is that as soon as you feel that uncomfortable sensation in your body—you know the one—when you think of a trigger, and your heart feels hollow, or your gut feels a big knot in it. Or your throat tightens up. Your skin gets clammy. You start seeing red. As soon as you become aware that you have this sensation, BREATHE. Breathe in through your nose to the count of four, hold your breath for the count of five, and then breathe out to the count of six. Whenever your exhale is longer than your inhale, it helps calm your nervous system. Be mindful of your breath and count if you need to. By the time you take five to ten breaths, the distressing physical sensations should have dissipated.

The next step is to start naming things. Look around the room. Describe the objects that you see. For example, "white ceiling, blue shoes, red carpet, soft fuzzy stuffed animal." Keep looking around the room and keep naming things.

Your breath helps you get out of the reactive state of your mind and into your thinking brain. Naming things around the room helps you get into the present moment. When you're having a reaction to a trigger, your body feels as if it is in the present moment. But the actual event is in the past. So, the goal is to get yourself into the present moment and realize you are safe. Naming things in the room gives your brain something to focus on in the present instead of being hypervigilant and reacting to threats that are not actually in front of you.

Another step I have added to this over the years is to repeat "I am safe, I am safe, I am safe" after getting into the present moment. It is my way of telling my reactive brain that it's okay to simmer down.

It is important to practice these techniques when you are not in crisis. Practice this multiple times a day. When you are in crisis, it is nearly impossible to connect with a technique that you haven't practiced. It is not yet second nature, so you miss out on the benefit of it. Practice when you don't need it, so it is available to you when you do need it.

Being on the receiving end of a betrayal of trust is a trauma. My life as I knew it changed in an instant. Post-Traumatic Stress Disorder (PTSD) is real. Trauma is trauma, regardless of whether someone else has had something far "worse." Comparing traumas is something we do to talk ourselves out of the intensity of our feelings. I remember trying to paint my own silver lining. "At least it's not as bad as (insert horrific trauma here)."

There is hope, though. I like to use the analogy that I found on Psych Central of a box with a ball in it, pressing on a pain button. It really gave me hope when I was in the thick of triggers and not handling them well. It gave me hope they would dissipate and not rule my life anymore. The visual of it is enough to stand out in my mind and imagine it when I do happen to have a trigger, even all these years later. Explaining this analogy to Nick helped him understand that triggers would eventually become less intense and less often.

There is a box with a big ball in it. On the side of the box is a pain button. When we first experience a trauma, the ball fills the entire space of the box and is constantly pressing right up against that pain button. So, we feel that pain almost all the time. As time passes and the healing process continues, the ball starts to shrink. But it is still bouncing around in that box, like those little ping pong balls in a lottery drawing before the numbered balls pop up. So, every now and then, the ball hits up against that pain button. Not as much as it did when the ball was completely full, but still will bounce up and hit that pain button. And when it presses that button, we feel the pain as if it was happening in that moment. We feel it and our nervous systems feel it. As the ball shrinks, it continues to bounce around, but now it hits up against the pain button less and less. Because it is smaller. And again, when it does press the button, it can hurt like the very first day, but it might last for a shorter time because the ball is in constant motion and leaves the button more quickly. This ball always remains, but the frequency of the ball hitting the pain button diminishes. And maybe the intensity of the pain diminishes because the ball isn't pressing the button as fully.

I have found great use for this visualization as I coach my clients dealing with various pain points and traumas.

Another important tool I used when navigating triggers was the H.A.L.T method. Triggers show up more readily and are much harder to handle when you are **H**ungry, **A**ngry, **L**onely, or **T**ired (H.A.L.T). This acronym was first developed to help addicts in recovery see when they were most vulnerable to relapse. But it's also helpful in other aspects of life, like work and home, and as luck would have it, for trigger awareness. Many therapists use the H.A.L.T. method to help their clients navigate circumstances in their lives.

A simple google search pulled up scores of therapy blogs discussing this model. Basically, if you can recognize when you are in any of these states of being, it gives you the opportunity to do something to avoid or alleviate the impact of a trigger. For example, sometimes when I become aware that I am having a trigger, I realize I am lonely. And just in the awareness that I am lonely, I can make a choice. I can either reach out to someone to connect, or I can ruminate in triggering thoughts. The same holds true for any of the other states of being. If I am feeling triggered and feel the sensation of my body reacting to my nervous system, and happen to be tired, then rather than going down the rabbit hole of thoughts, I can choose to lie down or meditate. If I am hungry, then I eat something. I do whatever I can to soothe myself so that triggers don't impact me as much. If I am in any of those four states of being, I do my best to resolve whatever is going on. Sometimes I simply don't have the physical or mental energy to deal with it, and I go and hibernate or play a game on my phone to distract myself and refocus my brain on something other than a perceived threat.

What I didn't know in the early days after I learned about the affair was that the triggers would not be in my face forever. The pain and the intensity of the triggers was temporary. The concept of an appropriate timeline for my healing was plain old garbage. Again, there is no timeline. There is no timeline for when the triggers will go away because we are all wired differently. We all have different experiences and different upbringings. (Note this repeated theme. I want to make sure you know this!) Forward movement is what is important.

Yet another of my defining moments for empowering myself was when I finally figured out that I alone was responsible for my own healing. No one was going to do that for me. No one outside of me could manage my trigger reactions. No one outside of me could love me enough to heal the pain inside of me. Only I could do that. It felt amazing when I finally learned how to regulate my own nervous system. When I empowered myself with taking responsibility for my own mental and physical well-being, without any resentment or feelings of victimhood,

I took back my ability to control my own path and my own destiny.

Back then, I had triggered self-hatred for my body. It would take a few years to heal my relationship with myself. In subsequent years, I explored inner child wounds and feminine wounds. Recognizing that my upbringing and culture lent itself to body shaming, feminine shaming, and sexuality shaming, it is no wonder that this experience opened up some pretty fucking gigantic wounds in me. It is no wonder that hating my body was a natural go-to response. This foundation had already been laid earlier in my life. It wasn't just the affair and the mistress wounds and triggers. This affair ripped open every single feminine wound I have had in this lifetime and in others. I had to open them up and light them up to feel the rage and intensity of emotions around them so I could identify what mattered most to me. This was the unveiling of generational and ancestral feminine wounds. These wounds were packaged up and laid out in front of me to sift through. To help me figure out what needed to be healed in me. This is what I lovingly call another poorly wrapped gift.

I ultimately learned that the things that truly light me up are the things that I need to fight for and use my voice for. This was about far more than just an affair. It was the beginning of me using my voice to talk about injustices women have endured for centuries. It was the beginning of me learning how to articulate what my soul is passionate about and the causes I choose to engage in. It was the beginning of me breaking my silence and standing up for women's rights and women's empowerment.

But before I could get there, I needed to go through a lot more processing, learning, and growth. My soul knew what I needed. So, I started my quest for the perfect counselor to help me reach my goals. I had no idea how many counselors I would meet and have to tell my story to over and over again, to finally get to someone who could help me start to heal in the way I needed.

Key Takeaways

1. Take a break when you're triggered so you can collect and ground yourself.
2. It is important to teach your brain how to feel safe.
3. It is okay to pace yourself with triggers. Don't be a martyr and face all of them all at once.
4. Become aware of when you are hungry, angry, lonely, or tired and use the H.A.L.T. method to make healthy choices while navigating triggers.
5. To ground yourself, try:
   a. Breathing using the 4-5-6 method
   b. Naming things in your surroundings
   c. Repeating to yourself, "I am safe. I am safe. I am safe."
   d. Practice these when you are not in crisis, so they are accessible when you need them.
6. Pain is temporary. As you learn how to regulate your nervous system, the triggers will fade.

CHAPTER 15

WORST
COUNSELOR EVER

At FIRST, I THOUGHT I was doing a great job navigating the betrayal. It wasn't my first time at this rodeo, and I had developed some pretty amazing self-help and nourishment tools over the years. During my first marriage, I read a ton of books and saw four different counselors. I took the helpful hints that each of them bestowed upon me, and I came into my own skin. I had done this once before. I could surely do this again. And I would be damn good at it. I've got experience, after all.

I also had Susanne, who I got to see and talk with every day. She didn't just engage in bashing him but also offered some really solid insight. Sure, the bashing helped. But we also had productive conversations about relationships in general, about human nature and natural tendencies. We discussed why men cheat and why women cheat. It was always an attempt to understand why people do what they do. And in understanding, I felt like I could heal more fully. Each morning, we would list three things we loved about our men. It helped redirect the bashing to something more loving at the end of the conversation. I was always looking for a reason to love him as I once had.

I didn't think I needed a counselor but strongly advised Nick to go. I wanted him to take a deep dive to places he hadn't gone before. I wanted him to learn how his upbringing and attachment styles affected his relationships, how to help me heal, and how to turn his life around. It was still yet to be determined whether we were even going to stay together at that point.

Initially, Nick went on his own, and it sounded like it was going well. I didn't know the specifics about what they discussed, but I trusted that the counselor was helping him get to his root issues. After all, why else would anyone go to a counselor?

But ultimately, I also needed guidance. I couldn't manage my life, let alone navigate the healing journey. The tools I had been using to navigate my triggers were failing me because of the concussion I gave myself. My brain was inflamed, my neurotransmitters were imbalanced, and I was in pain. Physical and emotional pain. As my pain level rose, my level of patience for any missteps diminished.

Add to that, that I was perimenopausal. My hormones were all over the place. Ladies, some of you can relate. On those days when PMS strikes, it is nearly impossible to will yourself into a good mood. Those are the days where you just want to run to your bed and hide under the covers. And as we know, when you are in perimenopause, those PMS days can strike anytime. But I was also raising four children. I had school activities, sports, meals. I used all of my energy to get the things done for my children that needed to get done. I needed help.

Counselor number one.

Let's refer to him by the initials BS (my passive aggressiveness at play here). He was probably one of the top two worst human beings I have ever met in the field of counseling. I had actually seen him when I was going through my divorce, and he had given me one piece of good advice that helped me release my need to provide evidence of my (then) husband's ongoing affair. Based on that, along with the fact that he was into astrology and knew something about Hindu deities, I considered him to be somewhat of a straight shooter and thought he could somehow help set Nick straight. I had no idea what his idea of helping a couple navigate an affair looked like.

It was all I could do to even get into the car to be driven there. My head was killing me. It burned nonstop. I was overly sensitive to lights and sounds. I had sunglasses on to diminish the impact of the overhead lights in his office on my brain.

We walked into the appointment together and sat down on the couch side by side, holding hands. I spoke in a soft voice because my head was pounding. I started with my plea for help with the triggers. "We are getting stuck in the midst of triggers. We need help figuring out how to navigate them, and how Nick can help me navigate them when they start." I spoke. "I need help."

I explained all about my triggers and our reactions to BS.

His response to me was something from a bad movie scene with a counselor who is clearly out of his own mind. It was like an SNL skit, only this was extremely harmful. He raised his voice and went in for the attack. He sat up in his chair, leaned forward, and fired off a series of questions. He asked me who I had been talking to about this, who had been planting ideas into my head, and what triggers could I possibly have? He said I was making the triggers up.

He threw out the fact that he has had six concussions, as if we were in some sort of twisted concussion contest, and he had absolutely no sympathy or empathy for the fact that having a mild traumatic brain injury actually makes it harder than hell to function in daily life. Let alone navigate a betrayal. Let alone withstand a verbal lashing from a counselor. He dismissed hormonal influences on the state of my mind and told me I was using that as an excuse for poor behavior. And he asked me what I expected, dating a man who's as good-looking as Nick. *Oh, okay sir. So, this is my fault for choosing a good-looking man? I should have known he would cheat on me?* Pardon my French. But *fuck you!*

He even tried to use my spiritual practices against me, accusing me of not having compassion for "those two." He was relentless. This misogynistic man did everything to gaslight a woman who was begging for help during her trauma. There is fight, flight, or freeze, and I simply froze. My nervous system had had more than enough. I stopped speaking. I stopped moving. I just froze. My breath turned shallow. My eyes glazed over. I sat there lifeless. I didn't utter another single word.

When Nick noticed my frozen state, he knew it was time to go. Nick cut the session short.

I kept myself together long enough to get to the parking lot, where I absolutely lost it. I broke down sobbing into Nick's arms. I could not stop crying. It felt like another betrayal on top of the betrayal I was already living through.

Nick decided not to go back to him after that. In his final phone call with BS, BS said to him, "I know trauma and I know drama. And this is drama." WOW. So now on top of adding another layer of trauma to me and gaslighting me, he planted an insidious seed into Nick's mind which would set us back again. I will never forget this complete lack of professionalism, empathy, and competence.

I have thought about this incident many times. I sometimes wonder why my nervous system chose to freeze instead of fight. Or fly. I felt like a helpless victim. I allowed it. Present-day Sujata would never let that happen. I would have absolutely spoken up for myself. I would have reported him to his professional licensing board, and I would have left reviews on every health professional site I could find. If I hadn't already experienced a betrayal before, his accusations might have made me feel like I was doing the wrong thing. I might have felt like I was not the spiritual being that I was because the human being in me wasn't ready to access compassion for anyone other than myself in those moments. The language, the pointed intensity of his accusations against me, the aggression, and the complete invalidation of my experience could have been the end of me in that state. But something in me knew better. Thank goodness.

Women's experiences are often invalidated by people who don't understand or who don't care to understand. Women are told they are making things up in their mind. Gaslighting at its best. Women's greatest gifts of emotions and deep ability to FEEL are often looked down on as hysteria. By men. Years ago, this "hysteria" was dealt with by giving frontal lobotomies to completely eradicate the emotional responses of women. It was the easiest way, besides thrashings, to control a woman.

When a woman who is strong and independent and has weathered many storms in life is begging for help in handling nonstop triggers that are bad enough to self-inflict a concussion, this is a response to a trauma that has impacted her to her core. It is more than "just" this wound. A good person and a competent therapist would dive deeper into why this is such a major trauma. Perhaps there are generational and ancestral wounds. Maybe there are things that have happened in her past that are being lit up like a raging fire. Perhaps this is the deepest she has ever loved in her entire life, and the pain of this particular heartbreak is far more than she can bear. And maybe, just maybe, she deserves to be believed when she desperately pleas for help.

Key Takeaways

1. Be sure to explore and understand the dynamics of how hormones, physical and mental pain, and other life events impact how you navigate your healing process.
2. Your experience is valid.
3. Being betrayed is a trauma, and triggers come from traumas. Your experience is real.
4. If you happen to come across a counselor who is not good for you, move on. You don't owe him or her anything. Get the help you need from someone who feels safe.

CHAPTER 16

INTUITION AND CLAIRVOYANCE

I MENTIONED MY GIFT OF CLAIRVOYANCE in part one of this book. I discovered it in college, and it accessed me during the months before my first marriage ended. I say it "accessed me" because I didn't really know what was happening. Before I took a good look at what it was, I called it intuition. But it was more than a gut feeling. It was more than energetically knowing something or feeling something. It was more than a hunch. I was having actual dreams and visions of people and activities that were going on outside of me. Consciously, I would never have thought that anything untoward was going on or that there were transgressions occurring or that my sense of safety and stability would be shattered. I wouldn't have remotely felt like my home was in danger of someone infiltrating it and causing damage. During that time with my first husband, my dreams were telling me all along that there was something I needed to be alerted to. But I simply didn't have time to go searching. And at that point in my life, I wasn't entirely confident about my gift or the messages from the Universe coming to me in my sleep.

After all of that played out, I prided myself on how I received messages and signs from the Universe and that I was plugged into them. I nurtured that gift and allowed myself to be led by the Universe. I was keen to the signs thrown in front of me and could confidently make decisions based on my intuition and the signs I was receiving. The Universe mainly showed me messages in my dreams. And while my dreams may not have specific characters, I could generally get an idea of what was happening behind the scenes.

My world changed on April 1. I felt like I was completely blindsided.

During the ordeal of me becoming crippled using an antibiotic, Nick showed up consistently. I believed we had progressed into a stable and secure relationship and that I could count on him as a life partner. It felt like we were solid. I wouldn't have thought, in a million years, that he would cheat on me.

So how in the world did I miss it? But more importantly, how the hell did the Universe and my own intuition fail me?

This was not a question I asked lightly. Along with feeling like the Universe didn't have my back, I felt like I failed myself. Abandoned myself. How could I not have had even an ounce of a clue that he was cheating on me right under my nose? I lost faith in myself. I lost trust in my own intuition and connection with the Universe. That connection felt severed. I lost the trust I had in myself to make decisions, to know what was right and what was wrong. I didn't trust myself to read someone's intentions. I questioned everything. At each turn, with even the smallest of life decisions, I looked outside of myself. I relied on Liz to talk me through searching for answers to life's simplest choices. I trusted her.

I kept asking, *how did I miss this one HUGE thing that was happening right in front of me?*

Well, first of all, he was a damn good liar.

Second, I did not miss it.

One evening, I was sitting with Nick and feeling down on myself. I was crying because I could not believe how terrifyingly difficult it was to make simple choices by myself. I couldn't believe that this is what my life had come to. I had been one of the most independent women I knew. And now I was relying on someone outside of me to help me make every single decision. Between my sobs, I kept asking how my intuition could fail me. How I missed this. I was derailed. The greatest gift I had was no longer something I believed in. I lost the wonderment I felt of the Universe and my place in it. I told him how mad I was at myself for missing it. I finally stopped asking and lost myself in my tears.

In the sliver of silence when I quit asking out loud, he quietly said, "You did not miss it."

HUH?!

He reminded me of a dream I had early on, probably a week after he began his affair.

I had awoken in the middle of the night, crying, breathing heavily. I was shaken. I had had a very vivid dream that he had had an affair. In the dream, it was him. Everything was laid out in front of me down to the color of hair this woman had. Nothing to interpret. Nothing to try to figure out. The characters were as they were in real life. The deed was as it was in real life. And my bodily reaction was as clear as could be.

As quickly as I told him about it, he convinced me that it was just a dream. Nothing real.

It was convenient, at the time, to believe it. I was just finding my way into a shit storm at that moment. I was a single mom of four kids, newly crippled from fluoroquinolones, and in a wheelchair. Most of my focus and energy was being spent on healing in every way I could. I didn't have time to go down any rabbit holes or even to think about the dream I had had. I allowed it to slip away from my consciousness as I continued trying to heal my body.

And now here I was. I had been tearing myself down, questioning everything I knew to be true about myself. I had misplaced my trust in my intuition and clairvoyance. As soon as he reminded me about that dream, it all came flooding back to me. I did have the gift. I DID know about it.

His reminder of that dream allowed me to start trusting myself again. I was able to start making little life choices without running them past my Liz for her validation and guidance. The realization that I did not, in fact, fail myself, was huge in this part of my recovery. I set the intention to never let myself to be talked out of my intuition or my dreams again. The failure was not me. It was not my intuition. The failure in this instance was in him.

How many times are we talked out of our own KNOW-ING? How many times do people tell us that we are making things up in our minds? It's called gaslighting, my friends. Our minds can get confused when we are receiving mixed messages. When our gut instincts are telling us one thing but someone outside of us is telling us something else, it is easy to believe what feels most convenient in the moment. It is easy to believe what we want to believe in order to preserve our sense of security and stability. Our minds choose that. It's okay. We are human.

I had to forgive myself for not following my intuition. I had to forgive myself for not seeing what was presented as clearly as day in my dreams. I had to give myself a lot of grace for where I was at that point in my life and why I chose to believe what was comfortable and convenient for me. It took a while. And since then, I have vowed to never let anyone ever talk me out of my intuition or my visions again. I am protective of my inner voice, and I will fight for it.

Sometimes it is hard to access intuition or to hear the whispers of the Universe. We must intentionally get still enough to be able to hear it. Or feel it. It is in all the cells of our bodies. When we are in great turmoil, it takes a little more effort to feel it because our minds get in the way. The internal chatter in our minds can be loud at times. It takes practice to hone the skill of hearing the whispers of the Universe. The trick is to get silent. I like to meditate to get to a place of stillness. Then I start asking the question.

"What do I need to know?"

And I listen to my body. As I tell my clients, the body always knows.

Key Takeaways

1. Trust your intuition. It is one of your most precious gifts.
2. Recognize the signs of gaslighting and stand in your power.
3. Keep giving yourself grace. Keep forgiving yourself.
4. Listen to your body.

CHAPTER 17

SHOULD I STAY, OR
SHOULD I GO?

WHEN DEALING WITH INFIDELITY, SOCIETY doesn't blatantly validate the choice to stay. Most TV shows and movies that portray infidelity inevitably end with the couple splitting up. The message is always that if you had an ounce of respect for yourself, you would leave. I get it. I really do.

But there is also a subset of people who choose to stay and work through the mess. It doesn't seem to be a popular choice, but there are many books, workshops, and resources available to those people who end up deciding to stay in the relationship.

One of my biggest challenges was making this decision. Early on, I did not trust my own judgment. I know that if I had made an emotional decision back then, I would have ejected immediately.

But that is not how I process things. Basically, I take care of myself first, get myself to a place of peace, then proceed. Maybe the whole "emotions will get you nowhere" thing is a bigger part of me than I realize. Maybe it is my Libra nature. Maybe it is the analytical, scientific side of my brain. Or maybe my life traumas paralyze me for a bit before I regain consciousness and start to resuscitate myself. I don't know which. But I don't make decisions from an emotional or angry place. I tend to wait until I have had a chance to collect data and information and then analyze it. My action is very deliberate. I choose to sit, breathe, collect information, and wait for the signs.

Any time I was ever at a crossroads in my life, or something big happened, I used this process. In fact, I used this process to go through every line in my divorce agreement, especially the child agreement part of it.

During this waiting period, I ask the Universe for tons of signs. I have learned to ask the Universe for big signs because in my confusion, I don't often recognize the little signs. I know this about myself. So, I ask daily. I recall asking the Universe for a big sign two months after my first husband's affair came out. I told the Universe that I was incapable of deciphering the little signs, so I needed something big. As soon as I asked for this, my oldest daughter, who was twelve years old at the time, walked into my bedroom. She matter-of-factly said, "You may think you're do-ing a good job keeping this from us. But we all know what Dad did. If I were you, I would divorce him." BAM!

So, you can see why I believe that the Universe will guide me and why I continue to ask for signs. Additionally, before going to sleep, I ask the Universe what it is that I need to know. I ask the Universe to show me through my dreams. And only when I feel that all the stars have aligned, and it feels right within my body, and all my dreams are pointing in the same direction, will I make a decision.

Sometimes I get lucky and other people make tough deci-sions for me. Like in my first marriage. He left.

But I did not make the decision of whether to stay with Nick or go lightly. We were only dating—it would have been the easiest thing to turn and run as fast as I could. In fact, Nick often told me that if it were his sister in this position, he would tell her to do just that. My brothers must have been chomping at the bit to tell me to run. But they didn't. They respected my process.

The part of me that observed the shift in Nick the night of April 1 could not ignore it. The part of me that still saw the cowboy on the slab of rock with the golden light shining behind him couldn't escape the nagging, gravitational pull toward him. Believe me. At the time, I had a vision board with a picture of that cowboy in the shining light. I looked at it, and I got so angry. In my fits of anger, I wanted to shred it to pieces. But something in me wouldn't allow it.

I don't know if a part of my decision was my fear of being alone. I don't know if my insecurities got the best of me. Or that I didn't want to start over with someone else. But making this decision was one of my biggest challenges that I have repeatedly questioned more than once along the way.

Some of my friends and family could not believe that I was even contemplating staying. After all, we had nothing together in the way of kids or assets. It could be a very clean break. While I asked my closest friend for her input on the simplest of life decisions, I didn't ask her about this major life decision. I knew what she would say: *Run fast.* But deep down, I wanted him. I read countless books and articles and did many google searches looking for others who had chosen to stay. I was basically looking for anything that would validate my deepest desire to stay with this man who I truly believed to be my soulmate from many lifetimes. Even though I knew it wouldn't be easy, I wanted validation that it would be worth it to put in the work with this man. But it was almost impossible to get silent enough to be able to hear the whispers of the Universe guiding me, as I was seething with anger. So, until I at least had a break from seething anger, I would keep myself in limbo.

As I look back on my journey, there were some definite moments that I consider to be big-shift moments. These were moments of clarity, mixed in with the turmoil, which allowed for major shifts in my perception, in my healing and in the way I looked at and processed things. These were moments that needed to happen to lead me to the next best choice on my healing path.

Deciding to stay

I asked the Universe for signs every single day. I asked myself multiple times a day if I should stay or if I should go. Wrestling with my deeply rooted insecurities and fear of abandonment, I wanted to do what I thought was strong. But I was confused. My heart oftentimes conflicted with what my mind was saying, and vice versa. My heart wanted to stay with him. The part of me that knew him in another lifetime and loved him dearly could not ignore that. On the rare occasion that I could quiet my mind for even a moment, I knew. I just knew. My heart felt him.

My core beliefs were another determining factor. I believe that we are here in this lifetime to work through issues that need to be resolved from past lifetimes. We are given similar experiences over and over until we work through them and learn what we are meant to learn. As we progress through various lifetimes, we have the opportunity to learn important lessons, resolve deep-rooted issues, and bring deep healing to our relationships. I thought about this and considered it carefully as I was making my decision. I could hit the eject button on this relationship and move onto the next without learning the lessons I was meant to tackle. I could wait until the next lifetime to revisit some of these same issues. Or I could stay here, with someone who wanted to evolve spiritually as well, and work through the difficulties now. I was stuck somewhere between my spiritual evolution and my human need to feel safe.

My mind wanted to make sure. My brain, specifically the amygdala, tasked with the responsibility of protecting me, was working overtime. It was telling me to run. My anger was telling me to run. But since I had given up my trust in my intuition, my heart and mind absolutely had to match up before I could decide. It was hard as hell to feel and see the signs I felt the Universe was putting out in front of me, especially in my state of fiery rage. I asked a lot of questions of the Universe. Mainly I pled for signs of what to do next. And then most of the time I would second-guess what I was seeing. My big questions remained.

How could I NOT leave him and still honor myself and not abandon myself? How would I rediscover my wholeness and parts of me that I didn't even know if I stayed with him? How exactly would that work?

For several years, I had one foot in and one foot out. I was ready to jump ship and run at any given moment. I was afraid to decide either way. The brain uses a ton of energy when it is stuck in limbo—that place where it knows it still has a major decision to make. I knew that, and I felt the weight of the decision hanging over me. I wanted to be in a place where I could confidently know that staying was the right thing to do. But in those early days, I was confused as hell. One day, staying felt like the right thing to do. The very next day, he could say or do something that had me questioning my own sanity. Inevitably those days would pass.

A part of me had to accept the fact that despite the big chance I was taking on this relationship, I could end up right back where I started with him. The truth is you can't prevent someone from making choices. No matter how angry you get or how many threats you make, their choices are theirs to make. He might cheat on me again. *Was I willing to take this chance?*

I knew one thing for certain: both of us would have to undergo a total metamorphosis for this to work. I would not thrive in the previous structure of the relationship. I would not thrive as the previous version of myself. And he would have to transform to be the man that not only I deserved, but the man he deserved to be as well. We both had to transform independently, then interdependently. And simultaneously. Our timelines might not exactly align, but if we were going to give this a whirl, we each had to be 100% committed to our own individual process and healing. As the process unfolded, we could then determine if we were a good match. That felt like a tall order.

I was, at times, clawing my way back to wholeness. In my ideal world, we would each be two whole people who come together to add to each other's happiness. I thought that's where we were when we started dating, but I had no way of knowing that midway through our relationship, we would each be broken into pieces. We would have to each assemble what pieces we still wanted to be a part of us to create a new wholeness. And then from there, figure out if we still fit. If we made sense together.

Why did I stay to even figure that much out? I had every reason to run.

After the big reveal, when we returned home from "vacation," he talked with my daughter and expressed a genuine remorse that "Old Nick" would not have ever been a part of. This is when we started referring to him as "Old Nick" versus "New Nick." And this was something I needed to hold onto—the awareness of what Old Nick was like so that I had something tangible to compare his new behaviors and patterns to.

I was tough on him. I didn't care about his feelings. I said things to him that I wouldn't say to my worst enemy and am, frankly, embarrassed to put it into writing. This Nick that was standing in front of me was somehow different. The old version of Nick would have never stood for what I was giving him. He would have turned and run as fast as he could.

But he took it. And he took it some more. He accepted my anger as part of the process, and as tough as it was, decided to work through it for however long it took me.

The more I saw New Nick emerging and Old Nick disappearing, the more my rational brain could fathom staying with this new person. But still, I needed more evidence. The shift on the night of the big reveal was one thing. But I needed to know how long that shift would last. Would he revert to his old patterns after the moment had passed? I wasn't going to knowingly enter back into the same scenario that we had been living in. I had to set new boundaries for the sake of my mental and physical health. For the sake of building something better and more solid than the house of cards we had before.

I set those new boundaries early on. There were things I was not willing to accept in our relationship. I looked back to see what, in his life, allowed such a slippery slope to exist and lead to an affair. One thing stood out to me. He had a group of friends who did shitty things. They were sexist and misogynists. They didn't value women and objectified them. I later learned that they hid information from me that they thought Nick would not want me to know. That adage that you become who you surround yourself with spoke loudly to me. I wasn't going to have any part of it.

Nick had a clear decision to make. He could continue to be friends with this less-than-stellar crowd, or he could commit to being a better version of himself. I equate it with a drug addict exclusively hanging out with other drug addicts. But when he decides he wants to get clean, he has a greater chance of succeeding if he eliminates being around the drug scene. It's nearly impossible to get clean and stay clean if you are still surrounding yourself with drugs and drug addicts. This same principle applied.

I set specific boundaries, and Nick had the freedom to choose what he wanted to do. It was clear in my mind that if he chose to respect what I needed at the time for my own psychological safety, then there might be a chance. If he chose to ignore my boundaries and find them unreasonable, then that was fine too. From that information, I could decide whether to stay or go. Because of my boundaries, his counselor (you know, the worst counselor ever) characterized me as controlling. But I was setting healthy boundaries as to what I was willing to accept. It was what I needed in the moment to establish some sort of psychological safety surrounding the affair. And again, I had no other ties to him. He could either agree to them or walk away. The choice was his. And my choice was mine. We each had the freedom to choose whatever we wanted.

Nick agreed to the boundaries I had set. Some of them included: no longer being around friends who contributed to his poor choices, not having one-on-one lunch or coffee meetings with women, not driving one-on-one with any woman in his car or hers to any meetings, being transparent with access to his phone and email records, and sharing his location with me so that I could see where he was at any given moment.

To me, these seemed like a reasonable way to start to develop a sense of security. If he could show me his willingness to honor these boundaries for a long duration of time, then I could fathom staying with him. For the sake of reference, over time (years), as I felt safe, I eased up on some of these boundaries.

About six weeks after the affair had been revealed, it just so happened that he was a groomsman at a friend's wedding. I was still in a state of shock and carried a lot of anger and sadness. Not only that, but I also felt frail. I felt like the fool that was the only one who didn't know what had been going on. Nick made the decision, a few days after the affair being revealed, that he was not going to Vegas for the bachelor party. He knew what the guys had planned (typical, raunchy Vegas bachelor party activities), and that would have been a deal breaker for me. Their activities were not something that were consistent with my values, and I was not going to budge on my stance. I never once brought the Vegas trip up to him. Nick proactively told me he was not going. That was a point in his favor.

However, his friends were not as happy about his decision. When we arrived at the rehearsal dinner for the wedding, I was a timid version of myself. But I slapped a half-smile on my face and made my way to the group. Every single one of them completely iced me. No one looked at me. No one spoke a word to me. One by one, they each walked away, leaving me standing there alone. Since Nick was in the wedding, I was on the sidelines. Everyone kept their distance from me. Afterward, they gathered at the bar area, talking and looking in my general direction. I felt self-conscious and devastated.

As the evening went on, I choked back my tears. I chalked it up to them all being assholes and told myself that I just needed to get through this evening. At one point, after I returned from the restroom, one of the guys had it out with me in front of Nick, offering unsolicited advice and telling me to get over it, or I would lose Nick. His voice was raised and accusatory. Like it was my fault that any of this happened, and I better be willing to do what I needed to keep Nick in my life. I ended the "conversation" by repeating "Fuck you!" over and over. I then turned and made a beeline to the car, where I finally broke down into a ball of tears. Nick followed closely behind me, having witnessed how incredibly cold-hearted his friends were and the impact it had on me. I think that is what confirmed that he was not surrounding himself with good people who were supporters of our relationship. And it was time to make the break.

As the weeks and months passed, Nick showed up to where I worked first thing in the morning, leaving dozens of roses at the front door for me to receive when I got there. There were many times when he showed up and wanted to talk to me. He promised me that he would make me the happiest woman in the world, and I would not regret the decision to stay with him. Those were some very emotional conversations.

There were times when I just stood there speechless. *Who was this man, dropping to his knees to plead with me?*

Those moments were impactful. Very impactful.

This was him, showing up, wanting to be a better man. A better version of himself. This was him showing up with humility, professing and committing to a spiritual path to his own wholeness. This was him desperately wanting a better life for himself and for everyone he loved. While simultaneously walking with me as I sought to heal and reveal myself.

I wanted him to succeed. Selfishly. Because underneath all the hurt and rage and resentment, I loved him. And I wanted him.

But while I was rooting for him, I was also rooting against him. I didn't want him to get too comfortable. I was afraid that if he felt like he was doing a good job, he would relax too much and stop evolving. I focused more on the things he was doing wrong, and very rarely acknowledged what he was doing right. I wasn't sure if he was making changes for himself or for me. So, I kept testing him.

He committed to meditation daily. He read books on all sorts of topics ranging from how to help your spouse heal from an affair to Michael Singer's *The Untethered Soul*. He listened to Eckhart Tolle, Wayne Dyer, and Oprah. He worked hard to integrate what he was learning. We had countless conversations about what he was learning and how it was impacting his life— not only with me, but also with his children. He was becoming a better version of a dad for them.

Several months after the big reveal, the weight of what was hanging over me was becoming cumbersome. I had to decide one way or another. And I knew that if I didn't make some sort of decision, then I wouldn't be working toward anything with him. It felt like I was wasting my time in limbo. I made the announcement that I would stay and attempt to work things out.

Making this decision felt good in the moment, but in the back of my mind, I reserved the right to change my mind. If something didn't pan out at any given moment, I could still run. The next few years turned out to be this back-and-forth level of commitment to give it all I had, and then pull back the throttle when I got scared. I got scared a lot. I had little to no tolerance for any sort of patterns that resembled Old Nick. Don't get me wrong. New Nick was showing up consistently. I pushed him past his limits. But he kept showing up. As with any pattern of growth, he showed up, stumbled at times, dusted off the dirt, and recommitted.

I like to use the analogy of learning to write with a non-dominant hand. It was like he had been right-handed all his life, and he was now learning to write with his left hand. Most of the time, he was aware enough to pick the pen up with his left hand. But every now and then because of deeply ingrained patterns and conditioning, the wiring of his brain, or just plain old being tired, he would pick the pen back up with his right hand. And you can bet that in those moments when he even just looked at his right hand and made the initial movement reaching toward that pen with his right hand, that I was immediately triggered. My hypervigilant amygdala would sense this threat in less than a split second, and I would be off-the-rails triggered. I had little to no tolerance or patience for old patterns. And I didn't quite know how to handle my triggers at that point.

Most of the time he picked up the pen with his right hand, it was him being defensive. Old Nick was defensive most of the time and dug his heels in the sand for anything I said that threatened who he thought he was. For example, if I asked him to meet a need of mine for more quality time, he would list all the times he had shown up for me. He would, at nauseum, point by point, tell me of the times he had been there, giving me his definition of quality time. From there, the conversation would derail. Because in that moment, I needed quality time, not evidence of when he had given it to me before based on his definitions of quality time.

I viewed any defensiveness on his part as Old Nick being in the room. And this generally happened when I had an unmet need or when I was being triggered. I know now that it was because he was triggered into feeling like he was not good enough. Or it sent him into his guilt and shame. His trigger reaction was to give me evidence that he was, indeed, enough. Unfortunately, that reminded me of Old Nick. And I hated Old Nick. So, this was a problem for me.

If we were going to stay together, I would be damned if we were going to return to old relationship patterns. I was NOT doing this treacherous work to end up in the same position I was in before the big reveal. Admittedly, this was my thought pattern when I thought I could control the narrative of how this would play out long term. I didn't know how much growth I still had ahead of me and how much surrendering to the process I would have to do.

Before the big reveal, I thought I was happy. But now I was transforming into a completely new woman. I had higher expectations for myself. I knew I deserved much more for myself. And I was going to have it. Since I didn't see it coming before, I was hypervigilant with any behavior patterns that didn't seem consistent with what I wanted in my life. Which explains why I had no compassion or understanding for him when he picked up the pen with his right hand.

But New Nick kept showing up. He showed up for me. He showed up for my children. He showed up for my mom and dad and my family. He kept choosing me. He kept working hard to change patterns of communication and learning to understand his own attachment styles. He even showed up when I needed to hear the echoes of my own voice repeated back to me during some difficult life moments. And he kept encouraging me to use my voice, even if it was something negative about him. He kept encouraging me not to silence myself because of my old, outdated limiting beliefs and patterns. At the expense of himself, he kept encouraging me to set my boundaries and not accept anything less than I deserved. His devotion to my evolution, regardless of how it played out for him, was one of the key reasons I ultimately committed to him.

The pendulum has since swung back to the middle ground. It took some really heavy lifting on my part to allow myself to dismantle the layers and layers of walls I had built around my heart. It took some time to rewire the part of my brain that questioned everything and didn't let any of the goodness in. It took me some time to come to terms with the fact that I was indeed taking a risk by staying with him. I COULD be on the receiving end of another affair. But I also came to terms with the fact that IF it happened again, I trusted myself enough to know the course of action I would take. That I would be more than okay. At any given moment in my life, I could choose something different.

I needed the freedom that these revelations allowed me to have. I needed to know that I would be okay, with or without him. When I realized this, I felt much more freedom in doing the work to stay with him. It took a lot of effort to allow myself to trust that what he was offering was real. My rational brain had to look and realize that anyone could fake something for a short time—let's say a year. But for someone to stick out the tough stuff for five to six years—there is no way he could fake that sort of commitment. No way in hell would Old Nick have stuck around for that long with the amount of hurt and anger that I was carrying. New Nick was in the house, and he was staying.

As I deciphered why *I* stayed, the truth is, I don't know why *he* stayed. I don't know why he kept working so hard to prove himself to me. I don't know why I was so important to him that he endured the years of triggers, anger, tears, explosive conversations. I have no idea. But he did.

Maybe it was the flickers of hope we would see and feel when we were having fun together or feeling connected. Maybe those moments were enough to know we would get there. Or that we could string more moments like this together. And have fewer angry moments. Somehow, we made the good feelings last longer and shrunk the in between tough stuff. Maybe we both just knew that we were meant to be together in this lifetime, as we had been in other lifetimes. And we were both willing to do the cosmic work that we were placed to do together. Maybe the gravitational pull was just too difficult to deny. But somehow, we got to a place where we feel content. And safe. And seen. And heard. And relevant. And loved.

But before all that happened, I had to figure out where New Sujata fit into the whole picture. This sort of thing changes a person. And that meant I had to figure out who I was and what was important to me. This wasn't as easy as it sounds.

Key Takeaways

1. You get to decide whether you stay or go. There is no shame in either choice.
2. Time and consistency are strong indicators of whether or not someone is committed to transforming.
3. When you know you will be okay with or without him, you free yourself up to make the choice that feels best.

CHAPTER 18

GRIEF

LEARNING ABOUT NEW SUJATA WAS not an easy process. I had a lot of work to do. For starters, I needed to process my grief.

Grief is the overwhelming sadness that we feel when we experience an event that changes our life in some way. It is something we feel in response to loss: of a loved one, of a relationship, of our health, or of the life we thought we had. It is natural to experience grief in the face of infidelity.

Grief is a complex topic, and I will go through the next chapters discussing the stages of grief. But first I want to talk a little about the perception that society has that there should be a timeline for how long it should last.

I think society is more lenient with some things like the death of a loved one. But even then, the people who are on the sidelines of grief make up some arbitrary time when they think the grieving person should move on. People have even less compassion for grief associated with a betrayal like cheating or the loss of a relationship. People are not comfortable with suffering, pain, and sadness. So instead of being there for people in their sadness, the natural inclination is to provide distractions and numbing. And well-meaning advice to "move on." Don't get me wrong. The intentions are amazingly heart centered. And I do think people in grief can benefit from taking a break from it and connecting with joy through their journey.

Because of society's discomfort with the process of grief, the grieving person can feel unsupported when the arbitrary grieving timeline has expired because most of the compassion and patience received from others also expires. It leaves the grieving person feeling very alone. She is left feeling isolated, invalidated, and dismissed. Those feelings on top of the grief can be unbearable.

As a grieving person, I did not want to be fixed. I wanted my experience to be validated, and I wanted to feel supported and loved. I wanted someone to hold space for me to feel my feelings, speak my feelings, and be with my feelings. Safely. For someone holding space, it means being there in that space with her, without judgment, without fixing words, without advice. It means being there with her, offering her empathy, offering her love. It means wrapping your arms around her when she is crying so she knows you are there. It means that you get comfortable sitting there with her, in her pain. And not trying to fix it or distract her. Holding space.

We have to be able to feel through the process in order to allow those feelings to pass through us and get us to the other side. I remember when I found out about my first husband's final affair. I was devastated. Within a few weeks, he suggested I was depressed (duh) and anxious (again, duh). He suggested I go to the doctor for prescriptions for antidepressant and anti-anxiety medications. I did it. I started them. The antidepressant made me feel like I had ants crawling around under my skin. I had a full-on panic attack. I could not step out of it. Not too long after that, I thought to myself, *Of course I am depressed. Of course,*

I am anxious. I didn't know how my life ahead looked, and I was sad as hell that the life I had was ending. Mostly, I was anxious about what would happen to my children. I wondered why in the world I was taking medications just to be able to deal with my husband when he came home. When I finally realized that he was the problem, not me, not my feelings, not my sadness or hurt, I stopped the meds and then was able to feel through everything and heal.

This most recent case was different. I chose to stay. In this case, I actually felt a deep heart and soul connection.

I am going to reiterate once again that there are cases that definitely warrant the use of medications to help manage depression and anxiety. *If you are having suicidal thoughts or finding it difficult to manage your life, please consult the help of a professional who can help you decide the best course of action.*

In her book, *On Death and Dying*, Elisabeth Kübler-Ross defines the stages of grief as

- Denial
- Anger
- Bargaining
- Depression
- Acceptance

These stages might not follow a linear path. Rather, people can jump from one stage to another and circle back around to a stage they already visited in no particular order. The stages of grief give us a framework to help understand where we are in our grief. When we understand where we are, we can better navigate our healing.

At the time, my sadness and grief felt insurmountable. There are many things to grieve when going through a betrayal.

When I felt stuck in my healing, I sat down and made a list of all the ways my life had changed and of all the things I was grieving:

- the death of the relationship.
- the reality that I thought I had. I felt like everything that he and I had shared was a lie.
- trust. I felt like someone had unplugged the security and stability I had found in him.
- the sense of innocence I once had.
- the purity of love that I thought we shared.
- the idea that I had someone who had my back.
- the loss of my very best friend.
- the loss of my love.
- the loss of light-heartedness, joy, and laughter.
- the loss of relationships I had with his family members when my pain became too uncomfortable for them.
- the confidence and pride I once had when I would walk into a room with him, hand in hand.
- feeling like someone adored me.
- my heart being wide open, accepting, and compassionate.
- trusting not only him, but all human beings.
- the confidence I had in myself, my body, my strength.
- how special I used to feel.
- the loss of my emotional and mental well-being.
- my desire to create a life where I shared the music inside of me.
- my sense of belonging.
- the illusions I had about our relationship.

- the things we used to do together that were filled with fun and laughter.
- the loss of the new family unit I thought we were building.
- the loss of what I thought our future looked like together.
- being able to go to the gym, as the location was a trigger for me.
- being able to go to restaurants because they were located in areas that served as triggers.
- being able to drive down the road without having a severe panic attack from seeing a car that looked like hers.
- being able to look in the mirror at my naked body without wanting to harm it.
- my life as it was before being poisoned by a fluoroquinolone antibiotic.
- all of my intense workouts.
- the songs I could no longer listen to and enjoy.
- the movies I could no longer watch without inducing panic attacks.
- the clear, optimistic, positive mindset I once had.
- sharing joyful holidays.
- celebrating his birthday joyfully.
- my plans for the future.
- the illusions I had of how magical our life would be.
- the magic I felt about how the Universe brought us together.
- the loss of excitement when I told our "how we met" story.
- the loss of my belief that soulmates existed.
- the loss of believing in unconditional love.
- the loss of me.

Once I made the list, I started looking at it to figure out what I wanted back and how I was going to get it. But first, I had to start moving through the stages of grief. I had no idea how I would manage all of this or how long it would take. And because the stages are not linear, I bounced around from one to another, and then back and forth, as if I were inside a pinball machine. But I will talk about them in order because I think it is important to understand what the stages look like.

Shock/Denial

There were times when I was just so overwhelmed by grief that I wanted to stop everything.

The word "shock" doesn't seem intense enough for how I felt when I learned about the affair. In the moment after I learned about it, I felt like I was in another world. Somewhere in between the world I was just living, and this new world that I would enter. It felt like a big void. Emptiness. COMPLETE confusion. Like something HUGE just happened. I heard the words, and I felt some anger, but still, in the back of my mind, it wasn't real.

Thank goodness for the shock. I firmly believe that being in shock protected me from integrating what was actually happening. This is what helped me to be able to drive my children another five hours on the day of the big reveal. I had to get into my car within moments to continue this drive. And I had to keep my head about me and avoid falling into a pit of intense emotions. Shock definitely served its purpose in those moments and throughout the process as I was uncovering and learning more.

Denial served me well too. I am convinced that my nervous system shielded me from complete overload by allowing me to be in stages of denial along the way. It is a protective mechanism that we, as humans, are lucky to have. As long as we don't get stuck there, that is.

I did not go through this stage and then move on and never return. In fact, I revisited this stage many times. Sometimes, shock moved quickly to anger. Sometimes denial moved to sadness. There was no predictability to it. But the comforting thing was that I knew this was a process. I understood the stages of grief. And as hard as it was through all of it, I knew that in due time, as I moved through my own process, that I would come out on the other side different. The challenge in my process wasn't that I didn't think I would move through it. The challenge was that Nick and I sometimes had differences in our understanding of how grief works and what to expect. At times, I felt like I had to fight for my right to grieve, go through the stages, and revisit stages at my own pace. After all, I was the one with the exhaustive list of things to grieve.

If I was only dealing with infidelity, it may have been easier. But life seemed to throw even more devastating events at me while I was healing. Things that made the infidelity seem trivial at the time (even though it wasn't). Just when I thought an affair was the worst thing I could deal with, I was faced with the diagnosis of an ultra-rare debilitating genetic disease for multiple family members. Now THIS was the most devastating thing I was facing, and it sidetracked me for a few years. This one threw me to the ground, stomped on me, swallowed me up and spit me out. Repeatedly.

What this means is that there was a period of time when my healing from the infidelity got placed on a backburner so I could figure out what the rare disease diagnosis meant to our family and how to proceed. This was not an easy task and continues to remain something I navigate daily. It sounds dramatic, as I write this. But believe me. It wasn't. It takes a lot to take a Badass Patel woman down. The diagnosis brought with it more shock, more denial. More grief. During the time surrounding the diagnosis, I needed Nick's support more than ever. He showed up. He helped lift me day after day. He helped me keep getting up and being the mother I needed to be for my children.

And of course, during this time, I got to deny that the infidelity wound still needed to be healed.

Someone wise once told me, "If it doesn't feel good yet, keep walking. You are still in the middle of it." I was definitely in the middle of it and had a long way to go.

In the next chapter, I will talk about anger. It gets its own chapter because of all the stigma that is associated with women feeling anger. It is a very real and necessary part of the process.

Key Takeaways

1. There is no timeline for grief.
2. Make a list of all the things you are grieving so you can work on each item along your healing journey.
3. The stages of grief do not go in order. It is common to move from one stage to another in no particular order. It is also common to revisit stages however many times you need to.
4. Shock and denial can help protect your nervous system from overload.

CHAPTER 19

ANGER

A S A PEOPLE PLEASER AND peace maker, my lifelong tendency was to make other people's poor behavior okay for them. I continually tapped into my well of compassion and made sure the people around me didn't feel bad for any wrongdoings. I rarely expressed anger. What this meant was that I often carried the burden of their poor behavior while they quickly released it. In doing so, I stored their toxic energy within every cell of my body.

When anger is stored in our bodies, it is the undertone of every other thing we do and every other interaction we have. It suppresses joy, connection, laughter, and living our purpose. Sure, we can survive. But we are not here to survive. We are here to thrive, live our most joyful lives, spread love, and connect. We can't do this when we have deeply stored anger in our bodies. Anger this deep has to find a way out. It has to be released.

After having my negative emotions silenced or frowned upon for much of my life, I have evolved over the course of my middle adulthood into a person who firmly believes in expressing emotions. If I had bottled up all the anger that was rising or put a nice ribbon on it as I tried to filter or downplay it for the sake of Nicks comfort, I would have exploded. When the anger came up, I had no problem with expressing it in whatever way it came out.

The intensity of my anger matched the depth of my pain. In Hindu philosophy, the divine feminine is the creator of all, as well as the destroyer. Kali is the goddess of death. In my personal life, there were many deaths happening simultaneously. And I was burning everything in my line of sight. Our relationship, dead. The trust and innocence of me, dead. The eternal optimist, dead. Everything was being destroyed by me, as a very real reaction to what was happening around me. And I didn't care.

Society looks down on anger, especially when women express it. It is frowned upon as being neither feminine nor becoming. Even worse, it is dismissed as being dramatic, emotional, hormonal, irrational, out of control, aggressive, combative, or just plain being a bitch.

The thing about anger is that it is often misunderstood. Anger is fear and sadness that is being masked by something that doesn't feel like it hurts as much. For me, the sadness was far too much to bear all at once. If I felt all of the sadness that was coming through my body right off the bat, my nervous system would have completely overloaded and snapped. I would have crumbled to the ground. My body, at some point, would have shut down into freeze mode. My expression of anger was a fight-or-flight reaction. It served an enormous purpose on my path. Because the sadness was far too great, anger helped me survive. It fueled me when I could have easily given up and sunk into the recesses of depression.

One thing I know about me is that when I am seething with anger and rage, I must honor it. I understand that in doing so, I might say things that could cause more harm to the situation or to the person. I understand that it could cause the breakup of a relationship. Some articles caution against expressing anger because it can trigger the other person's guilt and shame. I disagree. I expressed my anger to the people who caused my great sadness. Nick bore the brunt of my anger because he was with me most days. I did not get violent. However, I said what was on my mind, unfiltered, unedited, and raw. Whether he was triggered into his guilt and shame or responded with empathy, how he reacted was his choice.

I am a firm believer and supporter of the release of anger. I am also a supporter of releasing it in a healthy way. Violence against another person is not a part of healthy release. Healthier alternatives include talking, screaming into a pillow, yelling, kickboxing, working out, journaling, writing a grief letter, venting to a friend, or venting to the person who betrayed you.

The anger stage of grief is interesting because it is revisited often. I know I revisited it often and then bounced back and forth between some of the other stages. Each time I had a trigger, it would mostly culminate into anger. Why anger? Because the pain and sadness from the trigger were just too much for me to bear. My nervous system could not handle it AND I also needed to be a functioning mother of four children. I had to let my survival instincts kick in and protect me for the sake of what I needed to be for my children.

I released my anger so that I could get the poison out of my body and into the ether. It was meant to help me heal in the way I needed to. It was meant to express the immense, deep sadness in my body and soul that felt like could not be expressed in any other way. There was not an emotion or a set of words that was strong enough to adequately describe the immense pain that was in me. All of that came out as anger.

The person you are angry with can perceive it as a great many things, depending on their conditioning. Nick saw my anger as punishment, berating, chastising, retribution, maltreatment, and aggression. All these harsh vocabulary words that he had brought from his upbringing and perceptions turned my release of anger into something that felt punitive to him. Perception is everything.

As long as Nick viewed my expression of anger as retribution, he reacted with defensiveness. This only escalated the situation. Every. Damn. Time. As much of a believer as I am about releasing toxic emotions, his defensiveness added to the list of things I was angry about. It also didn't make a case to stay with him.

I had friends who could validate my feelings to a certain degree. But I tend to sometimes withhold the depth of my actual feelings from my friends. I like to appear like I have it all together. I like to show a healthy mindset. And I can step outside my heart and into my mind quite easily. When I talk about what rationally makes sense, it does make me look like I have it all together. But it doesn't help me heal because my deeper emotions need to come out. And I am busy hiding them. When I am in my head, the wall around my heart solidifies and keeps those emotions locked in my heart space, which then doesn't allow for feelings to come in or go out. That goes both ways. The wall around my heart keeps the negative emotions from flowing out and doesn't allow anything good, like joy or love, in.

Until Nick was able to understand to some degree what I was going through and understand what triggers were coming up for him, we would not be able to forge forward. I didn't know how to articulate that I needed him to validate my experience. So, I reacted out of anger and frustration, not only with him, but also with myself. It took a lot of therapy and a lot of conversations for us to be able to de-escalate in these situations and for Nick to understand and honor my needs.

Out of anger, I thought about getting back at Nick. But those thoughts of revenge lasted for about a second. I knew that having an affair to get back at him was not congruent with who I am. Nor would it help the situation. Getting someone back for the sake of revenge or hurting them is a recipe for disaster. If anything, it only promotes a sense of distrust between both people, and that will inevitably end the relationship or the hope of building something lasting and strong. Plus, it just seemed gross to me.

I would be remiss if I didn't talk about the anger I had toward the other woman. I was angry at the way she disclosed the affair, the details I didn't need, the names she called me. She knew full well what she was doing. The fact that she helped perpetuate a sexual relationship with him without giving me a second thought. The fact that she, herself, had been on the receiving end of an affair and yet offered it up to me. A woman waging war on another woman. Her venomous deceit and her lack of moral code. Oh, I was angry as hell with her too.

I was not graceful. I was not compassionate. I was not refined. I didn't even use proper grammar. I let it flow. I honored the anger in me, and I honored me. I had to get the poison out of my body and mind. When I say I let it flow, IT FLOWED. Earlier on, I had mentioned to someone that I wanted to do this, and they advised against it, saying that I would regret my choice later because this was not who I am. True, I am not anger. However, I am a self-aware, evolved, emotionally intelligent woman who knows it would do far more damage to me personally to stuff away the feelings, to temper them, or to filter them. I am a woman who is compassionate toward herself and honors her own feelings, even if no one else does. So, I did it. Three times. I sent three very descriptive and elaborate letters. And then I was done. It was out of me. Not once have I regretted it, and not once have I defined myself by it. It was part of the release and healing process, and I am ever so grateful that I was aware enough that I knew I had to do it. No regrets.

By the way, Nick was entirely supportive of this part of my process. I have to say that with my first husband, I did the same thing with my anger. He was not at all supportive of this part of the process because he loved the other woman. He wanted to protect her, and he wanted me to stay silent. His actions and intentions spoke for themselves. He was lined up on the other side of the fence with her. However, in this situation with Nick, I was very well supported by him with whatever I needed to do.

I don't care what society says. It is so important to find a healthy release of anger so that you don't carry the venomous poison around with you for the rest of your life. Anger gave me the courage to speak my truth. It gave me the courage to express myself, state what my needs were, and expect those needs to be met. If Nick didn't like any of my requests or who I was becoming, then it didn't matter. This event helped me understand that I could be me. And if he wanted to bail as I became me, then he had the option to leave the relationship.

During my angriest times, I viewed the world as angry and hostile. The world didn't feel like a safe place. Everywhere I turned, I saw people out to get one another and out to undermine me. It makes perfect sense that anger was all I could see around me. It is said that you can only see outside of you, whatever resides inside of you. For me, that was anger.

At the time, I thought anger was my power. And yes, it did help lift me up and helped me fight instead of giving up. It did help me survive when the pain from the deep sadness kept me immobilized. But ultimately, I worked through it and released most of it. And wouldn't you know it —once I released the anger inside of me, I could finally look at the world outside of me and see something better.

Back then, I expressed my anger to get the poison out of me. And anger was a mask for my deep sadness. But as I progressed through my process, I grew to look at anger in another way. I started asking myself what the anger was trying to teach me. *What about this situation, was I really angry about?* As it turns out, the anger I was feeling was also the anger I had with myself. For abandoning myself. For not loving myself enough. This anger was teaching me that I needed to love myself and speak up for myself. It was teaching me to get clear on what I wanted in my life. Through this process, anger became my teacher.

Key Takeaways

1. Anger masks fear and sadness.
2. Your anger needs to find a way out. Find healthy ways to release your anger. For example:
   a. Kickboxing
   b. Hitting a pillow
   c. Screaming into a pillow
   d. Journaling
   e. Writing a letter
   f. Counseling
3. Your anger is valid.
4. When you are angry, ask yourself what your anger is trying to teach you.

CHAPTER 20

BARGAINING AND SADNESS

Bargaining

ARGAINING IS THE STAGE WHERE you think "if only..." thoughts. It surprised me to hear myself saying things like, *if only I was better in bed. If only I had listened to my intuition. If only I had paid attention to the dream the Universe sent me telling me about his affair. If only I was skinnier, if only I was prettier, if only I was.... (You fill in the blank.)*

I was in a self-blaming mode, even though I knew that this affair was all about him. I don't think I believed that I was not all those things, but his betrayal sent a powerful message that I was not enough for him. At the time, I felt like I was never going to be enough of what he was looking for, despite him consistently telling me otherwise.

During this stage I often said to myself, or even out loud, *if only he would be this way or that way or do this or do that.... then I would feel safe.* At the time, I actually thought that he could fix my broken heart and all the other broken pieces of me. Little did I realize that:

1. He had his own broken pieces to fix, and

2. Only I could fix what didn't feel right within me.

Sadly, I didn't realize the second one for a while. I kept wanting him to fix himself, thinking that if he was absolutely perfect, then somehow, I would magically fall back in love with him, and all would be forgiven. During the months and a few years where I wanted him to fix himself so I could, in turn, be fixed, he sure did try. He tirelessly worked on himself, worked hard to understand what I wanted, how I wanted him to respond, how I wanted him to show up. He agreed to boundaries I had set up and guidelines that I don't think most men would even be willing to entertain. Not only did he agree to them, but he continued to live by them until I was ready to slowly start testing my strength in having some of those guidelines change.

Nick got a subscription to Audible Books and listened to the books on his commute to and from work. He listened to books about spiritual evolution, meditation, nonviolent communication, living your best life, helping your spouse heal from an affair, attachment styles, surrendering, and more. And the wonderful thing was he was integrating what he was learning. He was evolving. But his evolution wasn't fixing the parts of me that still felt deeply hurt.

It is true that without his participation, I would have had no other choice than to leave the relationship. He did help create an environment that felt safer by doing the work on himself and striving to be a better version of himself. But my delusion that he could possibly fix what was broken within me kept me stuck. In anger. In self-protection. In bargaining. In wanting him to fix me. In sadness.

In this bargaining stage, I also did a lot of superficial things in an effort to heal myself. For example, I thought, "If only my hair was shorter, I would feel better." So, I chopped off all my hair. "If only I had blonde highlights in my hair, I would feel better." So, I got lots of blonde highlights. I was attempting to be someone other than the Sujata who was deeply hurting. But those external things only lasted so long. About a day or two. Then I was back to the same old sadness that I just couldn't shake.

Sadness

Since anger is a mask for sadness, eventually, as the anger starts to fade, sadness will reveal itself. It was the deepest, most gut-wrenching, and emptiest sadness I could fathom. It was a deep void and a longing for connection and for the affair to be wiped clean. At times it was so overwhelming, I wanted to hit the eject button from life. I couldn't live for extended periods of time with that level of sadness, so instead of hitting eject, I bounced back and forth between sadness and anger. Anger allowed me to take a break from the devastating sadness I was feeling. And sadness allowed me to be vulnerable, to communicate, and to learn. At other times, I took myself back to the denial stage for a bit, just to give myself a minute to breathe. I did not do this intentionally. It was just part of the process of how the mind operates to help us survive and get through our challenging times.

Sadness came when I realized I had lost parts of the life I had. I felt like we had lost our spontaneous laughter and light-heartedness. I felt like we had lost the wonder of our relationship. I used to look at him with starry eyes. He described it as "You used to look at me like I was a king." I was absolutely smitten by him. And now, my eyes mostly showed disdain. And sadness. I was sad that we had lost the ability to be vulnerable with one another and share secrets that we only shared with each other. I wanted parts of our former life back. But I didn't want all of it back.

I wanted what I THOUGHT we had before the big reveal shattered it all. I wanted the potential of each of us.

For the longest time, I felt like the reality of what we had was a lie. I struggled with deciphering what about our former lives together was real and what was not. We were in a relationship where he was riddled with guilt, shame, unworthiness, and feelings of not being enough. Much of that conditioning came from betrayal that he experienced as a child. He never trusted the pure love I was pouring onto him. And if he didn't trust it, he sure as hell couldn't participate in it. Even though I had felt that my love could heal him, he could only let in the amount of love that he had for himself. He could only feel the amount of self-worth that he truly, deep down felt. And very importantly, he could only love me as much as he loved himself.

Whoa. I have to repeat that because it is so powerful. He could only love ME as much as he loved HIMSELF.

When your parents abandon you at age fourteen, you pretty much think that you weren't even enough for your own parents to love you....so how could anyone else possibly love you? How do you form healthy attachments when your role models didn't teach you or model it for you? When you are left to fend for yourself at such an early age and ultimately raise yourself, how can you ever learn to trust someone to help you or support you no matter what? How do you learn introspection? How can you dive deep into what has shaped you if no one sticks around or cares enough to hold your hand as you walk through it? You learn to fend for yourself, and you learn to do whatever it takes to survive.

During the months and several years after the affair was revealed, I was convinced everything we had was a lie. But as I reflect on it from my current frame of mind, our life was absolutely real. The love was real. The laughter was real. The sharing was real. We were where we were, based on all of the experiences life had given us. And it was very real. It just wasn't entirely what I thought it was.

My deepest sadness came from a disconnection from my SELF. My innocence, purity, joy, light-heartedness, ability to see the good in every situation all vanished. I felt like the compassionate and empathetic side of me had died. I felt like I had little to nothing to give to anyone outside of me. I felt like I couldn't trust a single soul, and that broke my heart. I felt like a bitter, middle-aged woman. I felt like the woman who used to love to have dance parties in the kitchen and sing with fake microphones around the house was dead. I felt like the woman who used to get up and look forward to the day was nowhere to be found. All I could feel was my deep, indescribable sadness, and it felt like I was in a pit that was so deep I would never get out of it.

After I gave myself a concussion, my ability to handle even the smallest things withered away. My anxiety and depression ran deep and the pit I had allowed myself to climb into didn't feel so safe. I knew I had to get help for it, and I did.

I want to stress yet again, if at any point during the grief of a betrayal you want to hurt yourself or idealize death, cannot function on a daily basis, cannot take care of yourself or your children, or cannot work, please, please seek professional help. I cannot emphasize this enough.

It is strength to ask for help.

You can get help in the form of your doctor, a therapist, and/ or a suicide hotline. I had spoken with my doctor, who knew the situation and prescribed an antidepressant that we both agreed on. There is no shame in seeking help or in using an antidepressant.

Key Takeaways

1. You are responsible for your sadness and working through it. No one outside of you can fix it for you.
2. There is strength in tears. There is strength in facing your sadness.
3. There is strength in asking for help. Find a counselor you like and trust who can help you through the grief process.

CHAPTER 21

ACCEPTANCE

ACCEPTANCE COMES IN STAGES, DEPENDING on how much there is to process. Because I was grieving a lengthy list of losses, it made sense that there were many things I had to come to terms with and accept along the way. As I walked my journey, I kept the list of things I was grieving close. I wanted to make sure I worked through each item on my list so I would have the best chance of healing. I moved through my grief, tackling items as I felt ready. It didn't all come at once. I picked and chose what I would work on. Eventually I moved to acceptance for most of what was on my list.

I accepted triggers as they appeared, knowing that they would potentially always be there as a part of my life. The more I resisted having triggers, the more they came, and the more they impacted my psychological and physical health. I could be resting comfortably minding my own business, and a trigger would suddenly come along out of the blue. The wind could blow a certain way, and a trigger would come gusting in. My body responded first, then my mind would weigh in. My mind would resist it. *WHY NOW?! Why, when I am having a good day?* The resistance I had to it made the whole episode harder to manage. There's that saying that what you resist persists. I can attest that this is the case. I would go through the grief process with each trigger: denial, anger, bargaining, sadness, and ultimately acceptance. But if I could somehow release the resistance to it, maybe I could move through the healing a bit faster.

If I could figure out how to let my triggers pass through quicker, then it would make sense that I would sustain less physiological and emotional damage. At the beginning, the triggers were nonstop. They hurt so badly that I feared them. Every trigger incited fear, anxiety, my heart beating out of my chest, anger, and sadness, which I quickly covered with more anger because I could not bear the weight of the sadness. I finally came to a point of acceptance that I would have triggers and that this was a normal part of experiencing and healing from a betrayal. I controlled my exposure to my triggers as I identified them, so that they wouldn't overload my nervous system, and I accepted them as a part of my life.

I accepted the fact that this happened. Ultimately, I reached a point of finding the reasons for this. I had spent years trying to justify why it should not have happened and wishing it would go away. But accepting the fact that it happened allowed a huge weight to be lifted off me. Resistance makes everything worse. It creates a heavier weight. And the way resistance shows up is not super helpful. Resistance to the affair showed up as anger, hostility, guarding myself, being irritable, and having a boatload of crippling anxiety. I couldn't function normally. Accepting that the affair happened and finding some of the positive things that came because of the big reveal helped me move toward greater healing.

This did not happen in one day. There wasn't a magical day that arrived when I accepted everything, and life went on. It has taken years to get to where I am. It's a process.

I came to accept that it wasn't about me and that I am more than enough. Yes, the message that the infidelity sent was powerful. It took a long time to accept the fact that I am enough. In fact, there are still times when I struggle with this. But deep down, I know I am enough. Now, it is much easier to come back to that knowledge in the rare instance that I have stepped away from it.

One of my game changers and accelerators in my healing was when I finally realized that he could not fix me. When I realized and accepted the fact that I was the only one who could heal me, mend me, love me, trust me, take care of me, and connect with my wholeness, my world started to change. And when my personal world started to change, our collective world started to change. My world went from constantly feeling like I was not enough, constantly pushing myself past my comfort in exposure to triggers, social situations, and continuing my mental exercise of how I could do better and be better, to me taking care of me. I committed to self-care. I started choosing me. Self-care has allowed me to continue to stand in my power. I had to choose myself and take care of myself or I would never thrive.

I accepted the fact that I didn't have to put on a happy face in front of my kids and hide everything that was going on inside of me. I accepted the fact that even as a mom, I had to take care of me first. Believe me, this one was a hard pill to swallow. I had most always put everyone else first. It seems to be a common thread among us mothers. Everyone else comes first. And if there was a time where I didn't put everyone else first, then I carried guilt about it. This time around, I accepted that I must take care of myself and do it without guilt and shame. Choosing myself has also helped me with the challenges of becoming an empty nester.

Even after deciding to stay with Nick, there were moments when I second-guessed my decision. Years passed and triggers came and went. His defensiveness came and went. Life got more overwhelming, and I built a progressively larger wall of self-preservation around me. I put the choice of whether or not I wanted to share my life with him back on the table. I could build a case for him or against him. As long as I was in battle with myself, the case was always against him. As long as the wall around my heart was sky high, the case was against him.

I started accepting whatever feelings came up whenever they came up as part of the healing process. I accepted that forgiveness was not a one-time thing. It is something I would revisit over and over and over. It was a process. I struggled with this. There are those who say it is godly to forgive and forget. But I could not forget. I could barely bring myself to even think about forgiving him. I wanted to. I wanted to be free of dying from the proverbial poison that I was drinking by holding out on forgiveness. I struggled with the popular definitions of forgiveness until I found one from Oprah that finally resonated: forgiveness is giving up the hope that the past would be different than it was. This really hit home when I needed it to. It kind of hit me like, *Oh my gosh. This is what I have been hoping for all along—that the past would change. That the past would be different than it actually was.* And once I accepted this definition of forgiveness, I accepted the past and I could continue my journey on the road to healing.

I accepted that healing was undoubtedly a journey that would take more than the original calculated time. I could stop my race to the finish line of healing and just ALLOW my process to unfold without the internal or external timelines and pressures I had placed upon myself. During the process, countless questions raced through my mind. I had so much self-doubt. Accepting that the healing would continue to take place over the course of my life in one form or another, I was able to finally start being gentle with myself and my healing process. As issues inevitably came up, I started being aware enough to realize they were coming up because those were the wounds that still needed to be loved and healed. And that was okay. There was nothing wrong with me. I didn't lose the healing race. There was no race to be run.

Accepting this took the anxiety out of the healing process and allowed me to just BE wherever I was. Also, accepting this meant that even if he had a different set of expectations for a timeline, I was not beating myself up over it. And I was not allowing his timeline to be mine. Once I got clear on it, I could help him understand what the true timeline was, which was nonexistent. I was able to be more compassionate by helping him understand that there was not going to be a moment when it was all over. Because this event was forever a part of the fabric of our relationship. It's funny, because once he embraced this idea, it was easier for me to be more solidly grounded with it as well. I could finally breathe with it.

I accepted that there was no way on earth that I could expect perfection from him. That was a huge one for me. When he promised to make my life so amazing that I would never regret staying with him, I believed him. And for me, it meant he would be perfect. In every way. But let's face it. He is a human being with so many conditioned beliefs and fifty plus years of viewing the world one way. How could I possibly expect him to be perfect as I defined it? His spiritual journey was just beginning, and as such, there would be many hiccups along the way.

Somewhere along the line, I eased up, and I started to accept that he was human, and that being in a relationship with another human would have its ups and downs. I can only imagine how it felt for him when I accepted his humanness. I am impressed with how long he walked with me demanding perfection. And I am thankful he kept going.

I accepted that while I had the dream that the Universe delivered to me, informing me of his transgressions, my illness from the antibiotic I had taken in 2014 distracted me. I would not have been able to handle such a blow back-to-back like that. The Universe dealt it out to me in a compassionate way, and I accepted that.

It took me much longer to accept going through the senseless toxicity from the antibiotic that robbed me of two years of living a quality life with my young children. I held out on that. And with that, I held on to a great deal of resentment for Nick. So, you can imagine that it was a surreal moment for me, just over four short years later, when I learned that some of my family members carried a gene for a debilitating ultra-rare disease. The disease affects muscles, mitochondria (energy centers of our cells) and the brain, some of the same parts that are affected by ciprofloxacin. Some of the similarities are uncanny, albeit also different. In my estimation, we could use some of the same modalities I used to recover to slow the progression of this awful disease. Looking back to when we received the diagnoses, I feel like I could have crumbled and stayed down (I DID crumble). I would have NEVER, in a million years, been able to rise from the news (I DID rise), were it not for my personal experience. It was the very weekend we received the multiple diagnoses that I finally accepted my fate from 2014, and I said out loud, "Thank GOD I went through the ciprofloxacin toxicity."

Key Takeaways

1. Acceptance is the final stage of grief and is accompanied by a sense of understanding and peace.
2. As you move through the stages of grief, refer back to the list of things you are grieving to see what you have accepted and what still needs attention.
3. Working on a long list of items to grieve can take years to accept. Be patient with yourself. Trust the process.

CHAPTER 22

INTIMACY AFTER THE AFFAIR

I T WOULDN'T BE UNUSUAL TO think that a chapter on intimacy was about sex. How do you have sex with the guy who betrayed you? How does that all play out? Yes, sex is part of it. But true intimacy is much more than just sex. Without true intimacy, people will never be satisfied with just the act of sex. Because in the mere act of sex, they are just searching for a deeper longing than they have the capacity to understand. If they think intimacy is just sex, they will be on a quest that will forever be unattainable.

True intimacy is about feeling safe and validated. It is about feeling a deep sense of closeness emotionally, physically, mentally, and spiritually. This is absolutely what I expect when I think of intimacy. When we sought counseling to work on our issues with intimacy, I was very clear on what this meant to me. Intimacy is not a code word for sex. It means that we are there for one another when the going gets tough in all areas of our lives. It means that we hold space for one another in the most loving and compassionate way to allow the other person to grow and process at their own pace. It means connecting on an intellectual level. It looks like us being able to discuss politics, religion, social injustices, and matters of the heart. It means sharing values and being vulnerable with one another. Intimacy is laughing and being silly together. It is being able to speak and be heard, as well as hearing him. It means feeling like I am in a safe environment to use my voice and know I will still be loved for my authenticity. Intimacy means connecting on a spiritual level. Being on some sort of spiritual path that points in the same direction. I have always felt that the purpose of being in a relationship is to help one another on their spiritual path. We may not be side by side at all times, but we walk with one another and support one another. That's intimacy.

In my ideal world, once all of those points of intimacy are met and supported, then the physical aspects of intimacy can create an explosive, joining of two to become one spiritual experience. Fireworks. BOOM.

Before the affair, I felt like we could attain my idealistic view of intimacy. I craved it. I felt like it was a part of my spiritual expansion. I knew he wasn't there spiritually, but I had high hopes. We attended a meditation retreat where he learned a lot of the same principles that I used to guide me. He had started meditating. He seemed to be on a path closer to mine, and with that, I imagined our intimacy growing. I enjoyed physical intimacy and wanted to be there with him. The big reveal changed that.

So how did this infidelity shatter my idealism about intimacy? And how did I get it back? First of all, I am still working to get it back. This is a challenging endeavor. I am not fully and consistently there yet. My view of physical intimacy has changed. With each passing day, I work to identify what's blocking my energy and what I can do to release it. Nick has evolved, and now shares my idealistic view of intimacy. When we are connected emotionally, we both do better individually. I still have some things to work through in this department, and much of my remaining work has to do with continuing to heal cultural and generational wounds. Baby steps.

The thing about this affair was that on all accounts, our shared perception was that I was simply not enough. It's no wonder. The message was loud and clear. While at the beginning, just after the big reveal, I knew in my heart of hearts that it had nothing to do with me, I let my own deeply rooted insecurities slowly creep in.

When I believed that I wasn't enough in the sexual realm, it was a huge challenge to convince myself that I was. But it extended to outside the bedroom too. It literally snowballed and extended to every single thing I did. I felt like I wasn't good enough in my career, in my financial successes, as a mother, as a daughter, as a sister. I didn't feel like I was good enough.

I started to become defensive and reactive. I felt judged and like I had to justify my own decisions. I didn't even recognize myself. Remember that journey I talked about? The one to self-abandonment and me being a shell of my former self? This was part of it. I questioned how I showed up in the relationship, subconsciously trying to convince Nick that I was good enough. I struggled with believing the positive things he was saying to me versus the messaging I was sending to myself about not being good enough. He already knew I was more than good enough. I was trying to convince myself that I was.

Physical intimacy became a BIG WHOPPING CHALLENGE. I questioned everything. *If what I was giving before was not enough, then how could he possibly be satisfied with what I was giving him now?* What seemed to matter was his perception or the narrative he formed around intimacy.

So how could I expect him to suddenly be satisfied with just me? After the big reveal, I gave far less and with far less enthusiasm. In fact, many sexual encounters were met with sobbing because of the images that would randomly pop into my head. How on earth could this encounter be satisfying to anyone involved? The truth is, it wasn't. He didn't want me to do anything I didn't want to do. But I didn't believe him. The part of me that thought I wasn't enough wanted to prove to him that I was. I placed a great deal of pressure on myself. I wanted to push through the triggers during sex to get to the other side. That didn't work. It was far too painful and created new wounds with each experience.

It took me years and a lot of inner work to fully integrate the new clear messages he was sending and for me to truly believe that I could say no and choose myself. And that that was more than enough. It took me years to believe that he was a transformed man that had changed his expectations for relationship. He had a new set of expectations, after years of self-reflection and introspection seeking to understand and integrate healthy relationship patterns. My walls of self-protection didn't allow me to let him in. I fought hard to keep those walls up. What I didn't know at the time was that for me, the disconnect was within my wiring and in my people pleasing tendencies. What kept me from reclaiming my power early on, besides the fact that I didn't trust him, was my own deeply rooted societal and cultural conditioning and views surrounding sex. I had a lot of deep diving to do in order to repair those deeply and damaging ingrained beliefs.

Not feeling good enough/self-doubt

It is clear that events surrounding the affair shattered my self-confidence and love of myself. Self-doubt was a huge challenge for me. And because of it, I somehow developed a strong dislike for myself. I could not look in the mirror. My physical and mental health suffered because of this. I created illness within my own body. And some really big questions came from this time period. *How could I be a sexual being if I didn't like my body? How could I express femininity if I rejected my body? How could I embrace the gifts I have and my creativity and joy if I looked down on the vessel for my spirit that is my body? How could I possibly contribute to anything positive or divine if I had animosity toward my temple?*

This wound opened up a huge can of worms. As I discussed in previous chapters, I grew up with body shaming, feminine shaming, and sex shaming. Culturally, women were not considered pure. I remember, when I was a teenage girl, coming home and my mother running downstairs to tell me not to come up. There was a priest there, and he could not be in the presence of a woman or even look at a woman. I had to hide myself. God forbid the priest sees the impurity of me, a female. In addition to this, I had a distant uncle who refused to eat at someone else's house because he didn't want to risk that his food was cooked by a woman on her period. There were countless times when it was very clear that women were considered to be second class. And dirty. While I fought this, I have carried some level of feminine shame for most of my life.

The infidelity just lit up that shame like a torch. It opened ancestral and real-life wounds I was already carrying. All of that poured out from the gash of betrayal. It was my job to sort out and heal one thing at a time, unraveling generations of ancestral beliefs and conditioning. Working through this and overcoming this took a great deal of introspection and courage to face. This was not an easy feat, given the repeated, reinforcing messages in every relationship I had ever been in that I was not enough.

As part of my self-doubt, I sought external validation of my experience, only I didn't know what it was called and why I needed it. For a long time, it caused a lot of conflict between us because I needed something I couldn't articulate, and Nick was living in his house of guilt. We picked this up years down the road with a counselor named Angel, who taught him how to validate my experience without it being a poor reflection on him. During this time, I also learned that it was enough for me to validate my own experience. It didn't matter what anyone outside of me thought. However, Nick was on board. This was one of the most healing moments that happened along the way. While it took a while to get there, it absolutely added to and was essential for intimacy.

Holding on to reasons to say no

My people pleasing tendencies and the internal pressure I placed upon myself were not something I consciously considered early on. But a few years later, the light bulb went on, and it changed something in me. I figured out that for me to be comfortable saying no to sex when I just didn't feel like it, I felt like I had to come up with something that seemed like a legitimate reason.

I had plenty of things to choose from. Past issues with sexuality, body and feminine shaming within my culture, sexual assault, past betrayals, infertility issues that essentially made sexual encounters failures, a bout of UTI that had me take an antibiotic that left me crippled and in a wheelchair that took me years to heal from, and more.

I had my share of issues that I claimed I hadn't been able to work through because life kept happening. And for this reason, I had a valid reason to say no. But when I took a good hard look at these things, I realized that I was actually holding on to those reasons as if I had to have them in order to say no. Somehow, my "unresolved" life experiences were legitimizing my choice to say no. As if I needed a reason. I couldn't believe the words coming out of my mouth when I was finally able to articulate what was unraveling in my brain. After all, I was a powerful, independent woman. I was raising my kids on my own. I made my own choices. But for some reason, this little tidbit of knowledge was holding me back.

This revelation and articulation of it were game changers. I could finally let all of my past issues go. I didn't have to keep holding onto things that hurt me in the past. I could own my power and say no to sex just because I didn't feel like it. Saying no is one thing. But saying no without guilt, and with putting my SELF and my SOUL first was empowering. Getting to this point took years. And some of my greatest healing surrounding my sexuality came from this revelation. Diving into the issues I had way before Nick came around was another key to intimacy. Being able to talk about these things openly and vulnerably created a deeper sense of intimacy than any act of sex could have.

As a side note, an interesting thing I have learned from talking with others who have been on the receiving end of an affair is that after learning of the affair, they tend to have an increase in their sex drive. I shared this experience. It sounds contrary to seething anger, but the two seem to coexist. I have thought about why this might happen, and I wonder if it has to do with an innate and primitive desire to couple with another person. At the most primal level, sex joins two people. And I wonder if that primal urge is meant to claim your person and somehow try to strengthen your bond. Like animals in nature staking their claim. I could be completely off on my hypothesis, but it's something to consider.

Forgiveness

There are books written on forgiveness. What it means, why to do it, and how to do it. But the books I read didn't resonate with me. I needed to FEEL it. I needed something to speak to me and the experience I was having with it. I needed something to really stand out as to why in the world I was holding on to not forgiving him. I didn't have the capacity to offer a magical confession-like forgiveness. I wasn't bound by religious dogma that guilts me into saying "I forgive you." I knew it would happen when the time was right. And not a moment sooner. If I said that I forgave him, I was going to damn well feel it.

I thought that forgiveness was all about him. Specifically, me forgiving him. For his transgressions, for his lies, for everything. And part of it was. As you have probably figured out, forgiveness wasn't something I did lightly. He apologized over and over, and I thanked him for his apology. I wasn't ready to forgive him. So, I just kept thanking him for his apology.

What it came down to was that I wanted the past to be something other than what it was. I wanted him to cast a divine light and wipe the past away. Only then could I cast an equivalent divine light and forgive him. Unrealistic, I know. But that's what I was able to decipher at some point on my healing journey. And as long as I held onto this vision, I held out on forgiveness.

Forgiveness came in spurts over small things. Baby steps to forgiveness. The more consistency he showed, the more comfortable I felt with forgiving him. It didn't come in one fell swoop. Each little dose of forgiveness felt like another tiny weight lifting off me. Something I could finally let go into the ether. There were many baby steps.

Holding out on forgiveness hurt me. It is said that holding onto anger is like taking poison and expecting the other person to die. This step still took a long time for me. I had to peel many layers off me, process countless wounds, get myself to a place where I could trust myself, and reach a point where I no longer wanted to punish him.

To experience true intimacy, I also had to forgive myself because I felt like I had betrayed myself. I felt like I didn't prioritize myself. I had mother guilt. I felt ashamed and embarrassed about my decision to stay with him. And for not knowing what I didn't know. I carried that for YEARS. It was like I took a double dose of poison and was waiting for us both to die. I came across a post on social media just at the right time that helped me forgive myself. The post read, "Be kind to past versions of yourself that didn't know the things you know now." Forgiveness for both of us was another profound key to intimacy.

Trust

Trust goes hand in hand with intimacy. Like any couple working through infidelity, it was the biggest challenge for us.

In the days and months after the big reveal, I was in discovery mode. I was searching to find congruencies or incongruencies so that my brain could wrap itself around the truths of what had happened. There were so many lies during the affair. I needed the truth, and I felt the only way I could get to it was by repeated, consistent patterns of transparency over a long period of time.

Nick was more than willing to be transparent. He answered questions I had, even when the answers were torturous for me. He agreed to and stuck with the boundaries I had spelled out, for as long as I needed the boundaries to be in place. He was willing to make those changes in order to show me he was all in.

The first counselor—you remember BS—had planted the seed in him that I was very controlling, and he shouldn't have to stand for that.

What I needed then was psychological safety. I needed it in a big way. I needed to know that Nick would be willing to do what I needed so that I could feel that psychological safety. It wasn't a permanent thing. But I needed consistency, transparency, and space to calm my mind and nervous system. At the time, it felt like it would never end. But the more congruency I saw with what he said he was doing and what I found on my own, the more I trusted him and the less I needed to check up on him. As my nervous system started to relax, so did some of the initial boundaries we had agreed to.

All of this had everything to do with physical intimacy. Because physical intimacy follows emotional, mental, and spiritual intimacy. For me. It just doesn't work the other way around.

Everyone is different, and I get that. And we all expect different levels of healing before we can fully participate in physical intimacy and have it be fulfilling. I expect a lot. I am a spiritual being having a human experience.

When it came down to it, another one of my biggest challenges was my level of intimacy with myself. It was in loving myself completely, in feeling safe within myself, and trusting myself.

It was in embracing the decisions and choices I had made in life. It was in dispelling the voices in my head that told me I wasn't successful enough or smart enough. I had to dive deep into my psyche to unravel and reassemble my own conditioned beliefs. I had to fight my old erroneous beliefs to convince myself that I was worthy and that I approved of myself. I absolutely had to become intimate with myself before I could ever extend that to Nick in a meaningful way.

Slowly, I started to regain trust in myself. I dismantled and healed inner child wounds, masculine wounds, and feminine wounds. And I regained trust in the Universe. It took me a long time to recognize this. But once I said it out loud, the Universe went back to showing me just how fully supported I am.

Perimenopause

I am in the editing stages of my book, and as I read the last sentence of the last paragraph above, I laughed out loud. Yes, the Universe fully supports me. We have done a lot of work to increase intimacy and try to establish a loving sex life. And then perimenopause kicks in. This is just another wrench thrown into the mix of all the various issues that have impacted my relationship with my femininity and sexuality.

As my hormones diminish, my innate desire for sex also declines. Now I have to rely on the largest sex organ of all, my brain, to drive that part of me. I am realizing that sex doesn't always occupy the largest part of my brain. In fact, it seems to come last on my list. If I am stressed, anxious, depressed, concerned, focused on a work project, focused on writing this book, getting things done around the house, taking care of people around me, then I have zero desire for sex. I also share less of my heart. My brain is already occupied, and I am left with no energy to conjure up that desire. Add to that, dealing with life stressors leaves me feeling physically exhausted, and I can't even keep up with the adventurous activities that we had grown to love and bond over.

Is this an issue for us? It has been the topic of many conversations, and I view them as opportunities to better understand each other. But with each conversation, little seeds of not being enough begin to re-emerge in my psyche. There are times when we talk about these issues, and neither one of us feels heard. And then we have these lightbulb moments when we finally open up enough to hear the other. I admit, when I am not feeling enough, I close off completely. I go into self-preservation. I want to run away. The triggers from the affair creep back up and I find myself not as prepared for them. It has been years, and I am not as hyper-aware of the deeper triggers in any given moment. But once I realize the trigger and how it is impacting me, then I start to do the work again. I connect back to the tools I learned years ago. I am glad I have a full toolbox. It takes a great deal of courage and bravery to let that wall come down and trust that we are in this together. Sometimes I dread bringing the topic back up because I love it when we are fun-loving and free. But alas, this is a part of us.

With each conversation we have, with each moment he shows up for me and meets me where I am, the intimacy between us grows again, and my brain softens up, releasing some of the stressors. Intimacy is a lot of work. But it is so worth being able to be vulnerable and connected to another human being.

Key Takeaways

1. Intimacy and sex are not the same thing. Focus on true intimacy and feeling safe first. Seek couple's counseling to help you identify what this means to you individually and as a couple.

2. You are enough. You are more than enough. An affair will light up your insecurities. But you are enough.

3. Forgiveness doesn't happen overnight. It is something you do over and over.

4. Transparency, boundaries, time, and consistency can help rebuild trust. Couples counseling can help determine what will work for you.

5. Ultimately, as walls come down, and you feel safe, being vulnerable is key to sharing intimacy.

CHAPTER 23

LESSONS FROM THE REST OF THE COUNSELORS

I N CHAPTER 11, I TALKED about our first couple's counselor (BS). He turned out to be someone who not only didn't help us on our healing path but created more damage. I have included this chapter about the rest of the counselors because each one of them helped me evolve in this very transformative process. They provided big-shift moments that propelled me (and us) to where we are today.

One of the hardest things for me was finding a counselor who I connected with and who I felt could help me heal. I had plenty of girlfriends who I could talk to, vent to, and cry. But I needed a deeper healing beyond surface talk therapy—something deeper spiritually, and on a relational level. I needed healing at the cellular level. I needed to feel it in my bones.

I needed help processing, wrapping my head around what forgiveness and trust could possibly look like for me, releasing the deep, deep fiery anger and keep it from settling into all the cells of my body (or at least get it moving out once it did settle), calming my mind, and managing triggers without wanting to scream and throw things. I wanted to feel peace again. I wanted to return to innocence. It seemed like a tall order, considering how long it took me to realize all the things I wanted.

So began my quest for someone who could support me through this journey and help me get back to "me."

I have changed the names of all the counselors.

Kara

I went to Kara for individual counseling. She was kind. And quiet. Kara listened to me speak, but that is mostly all she did. I heard myself tell my story over and over. My main challenge was still about getting through my triggers. I could feel the damage that was being done to my body, and I needed healthier ways to cope. Hoping she could help me; I talked about the fact that there were literally no books out there that dealt with triggers from an affair. She responded, "That would be your book!" Interestingly, I had not mentioned to her that I had thought about writing a book. She suggested this on her own. When she mentioned it, I thought to myself—*oh how intuitive of her to know that this is something I want to do!* But what do I do in the meantime?

The most valuable piece of information she provided to me was something I mentioned in the chapter about triggers. She is the counselor who introduced me to the H.A.L.T. method. It was at the end of one of our counseling sessions. She didn't speak much about it. She just wrote down "Hungry, Angry, Lonely, Tired" on a yellow post it and handed it to me. I googled the rest.

I was thankful for this tidbit of useful information. It helped me to know when I needed to actively avoid triggers. It also helped me to understand that I could be feeling a more intense reaction to a trigger just because I was hungry, angry, lonely, or tired. Working through the mental exercise of figuring out which of those states of being applied, I could more quickly get into my thinking brain and avoid going down a detrimental rabbit hole—and taking Nick with me. I saw Kara a handful of times before I realized that her style of very silent therapy and very little insight wasn't specifically what I needed as my journey unfolded.

Marge

Next up was Marge. I had asked Kara for a recommendation for a couple's counselor, and Kara thought she would be a good fit. Marge was a nice woman. She was older and had experience with couples dealing with and healing from affairs. As I looked around her office, I saw all the key books I had previously owned and read. That felt like a good sign.

I liked her because she held Nick accountable for his actions. And she seemed to have some empathy for me. It was clear that lack of communication was a huge factor in our inability to move through some of the sludge. So, most of the work we did with her revolved around improving our communication skills.

We focused much of our work on using "I" statements instead of "you" statements when talking. "You" statements are very inflammatory and a form of violent communication. It puts the recipient on the defense and breaks down channels of communication. An example of this would be "You don't care about me or my feelings." Or "You never tell me what you're feeling."

It is basically finger pointing and blaming in a somewhat aggressive way.

A gentler alternative to use when expressing feelings, is to use "I" statements. For example, "I feel frustrated when my feelings aren't heard." Or "I would love to know how you are feeling about this." We spent entire sessions phrasing sentences in these "I" statements. I appreciated the effort and the training.

However, I needed help articulating how I felt and to describe what was residing deep within me. I needed help trying to figure out what in the world was happening inside of me. And between us. It was nearly impossible to focus energy on identifying my feelings when I was spending all of my energy making sure I was constructing my sentences in the right way. It felt like we were in class and the teacher was right there, evaluating every single word that came out of our mouths. And there was a buzzer that went off if we even thought of the "wrong" word. I was so focused on the structure that I couldn't cultivate the content. It didn't leave much time for the depth of conversation and healing that we both needed.

We saw Marge a few more times before I felt a deep sense of not being heard. And it was hard to be heard when I didn't know what I wanted to have heard in the first place. I couldn't even articulate the fact that I wasn't feeling heard. Our time with Marge stopped feeling helpful and constructive. We stopped going to Marge.

Carrie

Next was Carrie. I saw her for individual therapy. I had met her at an alternative and holistic health care group meetup that I was a part of. She gave a terrific presentation on healing by feeling, and she had someone who had experienced trauma give a powerful testimonial. It felt like a sign from the Universe that I was there.

I made an appointment with her and felt like she really helped me hone in on the trauma wounds that were buried inside my body. She started off by telling me that the wounds I was working to heal had been there for a while. While Nick didn't cause the deeper wounds, his affair surely lit them up again. Which is why I felt like I was carrying the weight of the world. I became aware that I could not keep blaming Nick for everything that was wrong in my life. Carrie helped me make connections between my mind and body and actually helped me articulate what was happening. She made me use my words, even when I couldn't think of them. She helped me think harder and come up with something. Anything. She taught me more about regulating my dysregulated nervous system and how that would help me move through triggers. Carrie gave me hope for the first time that I would be able to move this shit out of my body. Through my work with her, I would be able to reset the baseline of my nervous system so I wouldn't be so close to fight or flight and live in a state of hypervigilance.

Her methods did not revolve around talk therapy. Her methods focused on the mind-body and were based on research that showed that a regulated nervous system facilitated healing from trauma. Carrie taught me skills that helped me become aware of triggers much sooner so I could get myself to the present moment much sooner. The more I practiced this, the more I was able to start engaging in life more joyfully.

Carrie also focused on the emotions that were stirring in my body by recognizing and naming them and then thinking back to the first time I had felt a similar feeling. Walking me through this process multiple times, she helped me identify wounds from my childhood. She helped me identify times when I felt not good enough, not safe, abandoned. She helped present-day Sujata go in there and soothe little girl Sujata. And in doing so, I was able to start the healing process of childhood wounds from a more regulated place. Healing the actual wounds from that place helped me heal every similar wound from that point forward. It was a powerful tool I learned, and it propelled my healing.

Going through this process with Carrie reminded me that I had a great resource already on my bookshelf at home. *The Body Keeps the Score*, by Bessel Van Der Kolk, had already taken up residence in my book collection because I had some yoga clients that wanted help using yoga and meditation to work through their traumas. I re-read the book and found it to be extremely helpful in working more wounds out of my body.

I felt like I finally had tools that I could use in moments of triggers, just for myself. This did not depend on Nick saying the right thing or doing the right thing. It was something I could do on my own, silently, without anyone even knowing it was happening. This felt like empowerment over my own health and well-being. The fact that I could be in a group of people experiencing a trigger, and completely calm my nervous system in the moment was incredible. It gave me control and power over my own nervous system, so I wasn't afraid to go out in the world.

Lynn

A few years later, I felt resentments creeping back in. A friend of mine who was going through a trauma had found Lynn as his counselor and spoke highly of her. He repeatedly told me that she reminded him of me. I thought to myself, who *better to help me than someone who is somewhat like me?* By this time, I was finally brave enough to say things that were uncomfortable. In the past, one of my tendencies was to work through everything in my mind. Rationally, I could talk through any crisis or issue, and it sounded like I had it all figured out. And I did. But only in my head.

When I first talked with Lynn, I was at the end of my rope. I knew I needed to preserve myself, and I had to be completely authentic with my feelings. I had to drop my resistance to being vulnerable and let her know I didn't have it all figured out. I needed help bringing out and verbalizing the tougher stuff that wasn't so neat and tidy.

She helped me do this. She asked probing questions, and I was honest with myself. I realized that my physical and mental health was suffering because of things that were left unsaid, which led to more resentment than anyone in a relationship should have. No relationship could thrive with the amount of resentment I was still carrying. I reached a crossroads. Either our relationship had to change again, or I would have to ditch the relationship and save myself. Being able to say the unsaid was like lifting off a two-ton weight every time we met. I felt incredibly liberated in finally putting words to these not-so-pretty feelings and not having to sugar-coat or filter it within me. I was finally able to admit what had been living inside of me and weighing me down.

As I was figuring out some deeper truths about my daily life with Nick, we reached what seemed to be an impasse. He kept asking me to try couple's counseling again, and I refused. I was tired of all the counselors we had met with who didn't seem to understand what I needed. I was tired of not being seen or heard and having my experience invalidated or overlooked. I was tired of telling the same old story over and over, hoping for resolution but being met with more questions than answers. And truthfully, I had one foot out and was ready to run.

That summer, we went on vacation, and Nick was talking to me about something that was making him sad. Nothing about me whatsoever. His own personal sadness. In that moment, I felt zero compassion. I felt zero empathy. I offered zero percent of my heart to support him. And in the days and weeks following that, I gained the clarity I needed to make my next best choice.

The clarity—my defining moments in recovering my SELF

What became evident to me was that I had lost the essence of who I am as a person. I have always prided myself on being a loving, compassionate individual. If someone is suffering, I am there. I can put anything aside to support or help someone in crisis or in pain.

Another major moment of clarity was that I was finally able to articulate that I had lost my innocence, and more importantly, that I so badly wanted it back. My family may joke about my innocence, but I cherish the five-year-old little girl in me who sees wonder and goodness in the world. I wanted to reconnect with her.

I also discovered that I felt anxious every single day when it was time for Nick to come home. I had to meditate for half an hour before he came home, and even then, I would brace myself for whatever our interaction would be. I felt like I was always on defense. I felt like he had expectations of me that I simply did not want to deliver. I felt like if I delivered, then I was not being true to myself. I was betraying myself. And my self-betrayal had finally gotten the best of my mental and physical health. I was completely depleted, and self-betrayal and self-sacrifice were no longer an option. That's clarity.

Lynn encouraged me to go to couple's counseling one more time and just gather information. I knew I would be okay with or without him. But I definitely had to find myself, peel off the layers of pain that I was wrapped in and make some tough decisions.

I only make decisions from a place of peace, so I agreed.

Angel

In comes Angel. Angel was a godsend. Nick and I arrived with our defenses up. I had wrapped several layers of bricks around my heart. And so had he. I was determined not to let anything in, good or bad. During that first session, she asked us to tell her about how we met and got together. Nick and I told the story, feeding off each other, finishing each other's sentences and taking turns filling in the gaps. For the first time in years, I felt a sense of serendipity about our relationship again. And as we continued to show up week after week, we rediscovered the love that was buried deep within our years of pain, resentment, conflict, and experiences. We discovered a new love. A more stable, nurturing, nourishing, and comforting love between us. We let our defenses come down one brick at a time and realized that we both wanted to be on the same side of the fence, together. I noticed that once Nick decided to open his heart, he could do so like flipping a switch. I was impressed at his ability to do this. I didn't have this skill. I opened mine much more slowly.

Angel took the time to extract what each of us was feeling at any given moment and made sure we took the time to do a deep dive into whatever that was. She SAW and HEARD me. And she was compassionate and gentle in her approach to helping Nick see and hear what she was seeing and hearing from me. Angel also SAW and HEARD Nick and she was able to help me see and hear him. It was through our work together that I heard Nick for the first time in a long time. I heard his love come through. I heard his compassion and his remorse. I heard his true, deep desire to continue to evolve into the best version of himself. I heard him repeat statements he had made in years past. But this time I heard more than just his words. I FINAL-LY HEARD HIM and felt his heart and let it in.

Through our work together, I realized I had been holding onto my walls of protection. It was like holding onto the bow of a sinking ship for dear life. It would take me under eventually, but at the moment, I thought it was keeping me afloat on top of the water. I thought it was keeping me safe. My nervous system had become extremely hypervigilant again, and I couldn't tell the difference between my hypervigilance and my intuition. In my steadfastness to not abandon my intuition, I was actually holding onto my hypervigilance as well. I had some personal work to do. Which I did. In the form of MORE inner child work, feminine and masculine wound work, affirmations, and more. I realized my physical health had taken its toll from the messages I had sent myself and received, and from not letting love in.

Angel supported the work I was doing on my own, and she asked insightful questions that gave me reason for self-reflection and deeper understanding. It is through this whole process that I finally felt deep peace within my soul. I finally felt safe to allow my heart to feel joy. This is a continual process, and I still set intentions to connect with joy and to allow Nick's love in daily.

The span of this line of counselors was six years. Yes, six. It hasn't been easy. Many people do not choose to stay with the one who betrays them. Both staying and leaving are tough. There truly is no easy road. It certainly is not an overnight fix or something you just get over. This becomes part of the fabric of your being and of your relationship.

I had no idea that it would take me years to finally feel a level of profound peace. But realistically, it takes years to do the amount of internal work I have done to get to where I am. The work continues. Naturally, new challenges emerge as life continues to unfold. But from where I am, and where we are as a couple, we are much better equipped to navigate those challenges.

The line of counselors had to happen, and I am so thankful I did not throw in the towel. With each counselor, I learned something valuable, which turned out to be the next step on this journey. I could not have jumped from step one to the final step. Each step along the way, and each personality I or we interacted with, provided us with either a tool or the clarity we needed to make the next best choice.

Healing is not a linear path. It is a jagged path that trends upward. It is okay to work with a counselor until they have imparted what they can, and then to move on to someone else who can propel your healing to the next level. If you're lucky, you find someone like Angel, who I think I could hang with for a long while. Everyone has different areas of expertise and interests. It's important to find someone who matches the energetic frequency that feels good to you. Ultimately, the level and depth of healing comes down to doing personal work every single day. Outside of the office.

Key Takeaways

1. Find a counselor that you feel comfortable with and resonates with you.
2. It is okay to move through various counselors until you find the one you like.
3. If you are seeing a counselor who you do not feel comfortable with, move on. You don't owe them anything.
4. We are sent to specific counselors for a reason. Find the reason and lessons learned from each counselor and add to it.
5. Your journey is yours. Healing is a jagged path.
6. Do the work outside the counselor's office. That's where the real work lies.

PART 3

The Transformation

Butterfly

Part three of this book is about the transformation. It is about the reflections and realizations that allowed me to realign with the truth of me. It is about the rebirth of me, after a very painful death of life as it once was. It is about how I found my truth, what propelled me on my path, and some deep realizations that had to come through to me. It is about me choosing me. Transformation is about how I got my wings to fly again.

CHAPTER 24

PERMISSION TO CHOOSE EASE AND INNOCENCE

Choosing ease

FOR MOST OF MY ADULT life, whenever there was struggle in my life, I followed the Buddhist principle of leaning into the pain. Through my spiritual evolution and practices, I was taught to lean in and feel the pain. Don't' resist what is happening. Resistance will only make it worse. So instead of running and hiding from pain, just lean in. Because when we look our pain and suffering in the eyes, we bring light to it. When we bring enough light to it, darkness has nowhere to live. And voilà, our suffering and pain start to dissipate. Easy breezy.

Well, my handling of pain from this trauma was no different. I kept the Buddhist philosophy close in my mind and leaned into the pain. And then I leaned in further. There was a LOT to lean into. I thought I had to face every pain and lean into every suffering and face every resistance and every trigger. No matter how fast they were coming at me, and no matter how intense the pain was. I thought that if I were truly going to "succeed" on this spiritual path of growth and expansion, then I totally needed to lean all the way in. I am all about the spiritual journey. In fact, I tend to be an overachiever in this area. I figured leaning in would make me face all of it all at once and accelerate my healing path and my path to enlightenment. This would help me propel to the next level of my existence. I felt like I had many missions to accomplish in life, and this was another one of those challenges that I would conquer in the quickest way possible. This turned out to be flawed thinking.

The constant leaning into pain, triggers, and suffering overwhelmed my nervous system. For months, I found it hard to function because I kept deliberately choosing to lean in, which meant I was deliberately choosing to overwhelm my nervous system on a daily basis. Overwhelm to my nervous system manifested as anxiety, depression, irritability and having a short fuse. It meant feeling an underlying sense of unrest and discomfort to my core. I didn't trust myself to be in a stressful situation for fear of imploding.

One day, I sat down to meditate and as always, set my intentions for peace. This day didn't seem any different from all the other days I asked for it. Sooner or later, I would manifest peace. It was just a matter of time. On this day, however, I heard the whisper of the Universe. *Choose ease.*

WHOA!

To rephrase that, I am allowed to say NO to discomfort.

Wait, what? I thought to myself.

I am allowed to say NO to discomfort? I am allowed to choose ease?

It occurred to me that I wasn't following my own advice I give to my yoga students. I encourage them to make modifications to yoga poses, to honor their bodies, and choose comfort over discomfort. I needed this. This whisper of the Universe taught me something that would bring me great peace.

I didn't have to lean into pain and suffering.

I could simply let go and lean into joy. And lean into love. And lean into the EASE of life. Today, more often than not, I am finally giving myself permission to choose EASE. To not lean into the pain. To say no to toxic people and experiences, uncomfortable conversations I am not ready for, and watching movies that trigger the hell out of me. Anytime that my body starts to feel uneasy, I am allowed to eject. I am allowed to say no. I am allowed to lean into the innocence of my inner child. And I am allowed to go to my inner child, who is huddled up, crying, "Oh my God, not this again!" and say, "You know what? I've got you. Let's go to this field of rainbows and butterflies and check that out instead."

Choosing innocence

As you know, I have historically been abnormally innocent and naive, despite some of the shitty experiences life has thrown at me.

As I was processing and healing from the infidelity, there was a point when I was having an extremely difficult time pinpointing exactly what was missing from my sense of who I am. I was functioning okay, managing triggers, going out with friends, and taking care of myself. I was connecting with some joy and even finding moments of laughter. But there was still this huge gaping void inside of me. I had lost a very important part of my essence, and I felt it.

I felt bitter. I felt like I couldn't fully trust anyone. It was like I was sleeping with one eye open. *When would the other shoe drop? When would my life completely fall apart again?* It is best not to get too comfortable or too joyful because when (not if) the other shoe dropped, I would have less of a distance to fall to the ground. It was inevitable that I would fall, so I protected myself by not letting true joy in. I was constantly bracing for that fall.

It wasn't until one day when I was re-reading the list of everything I had been grieving through this betrayal that I finally figured it out. As I went down the list, I assessed whether or not I had properly grieved each thing. I placed checkmarks next to the items that I thought I had done a good job processing. When I was done, the one glaring item that didn't have a checkmark next to it was the loss of my innocence. The loss of being in awe and wonder of the world. The innocence that allowed me to meet someone new and think the best of them. I had lost my trust in the Universe.

Some of the things that I had grieved, I knew I couldn't get back. Some of them I didn't want back. But this one, well I wanted it.

In that moment, I said it out loud. *I lost my innocence, and damnit, I want it back!*

Was it possible to get that back? After all I had been through?

When I make a decision and set my mind on something, I achieve it. It is a matter of saying what I want and then setting the wheels in motion to get it. It's called setting an intention. It is planting a fertile seed in the soil of the Universe, detaching from the outcome, and allowing the Universe to do the rest.

I spent the greater part of the afternoon thinking about it, meditating on it, visualizing how it would be if I were able to get my innocence back. I recalled times in my life when I had the gift of innocence and how amazing it felt. I felt it in my heart. And then I remembered a picture of my five-year-old, wide-eyed, innocent self that hangs in my living room. I ran down the steps to look. When I looked at it, I instantly felt it. I felt the innocence of that little girl. And I felt the lack of it at the same time. I cried as I realized how badly I wanted it back, and how much I didn't want to feel bitter anymore.

But how could I get that feeling back and have it actually stick with me?

I decided to take a picture of it and make it my lock screen photo on my phone. Every time I looked at my phone (let's face it, probably one hundred times a day), it reminded me to choose innocence. It reminded me of how I wanted to feel, what I wanted to be and what I wanted to have. It reminded me to continuously set the intention to return to innocence.

This was huge. It was the next piece I needed to connect back with the authentic parts of me that allowed me to feel joy. It was important to me.

I have received many jokes and people have struggled to understand how I could choose to reclaim my innocence when I "should be" protecting myself. I have people who love me who try to protect me and teach me the (harsh) ways of the world.

I think most people cannot fathom the goodness that resides in me and the purity of thought that I can come from. But I also have a very keen, innate alarm system that goes off if I feel like I am in physical danger, or something doesn't seem right. I rely on that system when I really need to be alerted.

In choosing innocence, I am not turning a blind eye. I still care about social issues. Women's rights issues fire me up. Racism and injustices light me up. I attend marches to draw attention to some of those causes. I abhor abuse, oppression, injustices, misogyny, and racism.

But in my personal life, in relationships, I prefer innocence. Reclaiming my innocence means that I am free to engage in authentic relationships with people. I am free to be my gregarious, "easy laugh" self who doesn't hold back innocent physical touch for fear of giving the wrong impression. I am free to compliment men and women alike and be genuine in those compliments. I can express my love and admiration for my male friends from a place of innocence and authenticity without regard for how anyone might misinterpret my words. Because that's just the way I think.

In choosing innocence, I think I am at a happy medium right now. There are still moments when I feel anxious for what's about to happen or depressed about the way I wish things were. But I also have moments where I am connected to my innocence, and I like that.

I have boundaries. If I am clear within myself about my boundaries and values, I am good. What this means is that I get to live with a more open heart. And that just feels better to me.

I get to choose my innocent life and perspective, where I get to be genuine and not have to hold back admiration and hugs just because the world has become a cynical place. I get to choose this.

And guess what—you're allowed to choose ease and innocence too. Meet me in that field of rainbows, flowers, and butterflies. It is absolutely beautiful there.

Key Takeaways

1. You are allowed to choose ease. Choose comfort over discomfort.
2. Listen to your body. It always knows.
3. You are allowed to say no to people and situations that disrupt your peace. Set boundaries and take care of yourself.

CHAPTER 25

THE OTHER WOMAN

I T IS IMPORTANT TO TALK about the other woman. Not because she is significant, but because she can be an overwhelming center of focus of anger for those of us who have been cheated on.

Early on, I was beyond angry at the other woman. I knew her, and it baffled me how a woman could do this to another woman. I told my friend that I was angry at the other woman and was surprised by my friend's immediate rebuttal. She, being way angrier at Nick than I was at that moment, dismissed the conversation I wanted to have and told me that the other woman was not the one who betrayed me and that I did not have a relationship with her. And then unleashed on Nick. When I looked back on our conversation later, I understood where she was coming from. I understood her level of care for me and her desire to be there for me. She's a great friend. But I carried that initial conversation with me for a long time, questioning whether or not my anger was misplaced and feeling alone in that.

You have to go through something like this to understand what goes through our minds. I have supported other friends who have been on the receiving end of betrayal in the form of an affair. Having gone through it multiple times, I completely understand the desire for revenge. I understand the name-calling, character defamation, wanting to throw her under every bus, and making her out to be a cheap prostitute. (I found my most creative use of words during those first forty-eight hours after learning about the affair. I used words and phrases that I didn't even know I knew!) I understand wanting her to suffer. I understand the pointed anger at this other woman who KNEW the man was in a relationship. *How could she?! How could she do this to me?*

I am going to attempt to answer that question.

The first morning during a recent trip to Turks and Caicos, I woke up early and went to the beach before anyone else was out there. This, in and of itself, was a feat. I was never the first one out. The sun was just beginning to rise, and the waves were crashing onto the beach like a lullaby. I found a secluded spot where I could lay my towel out and settle in for some long-awaited beach yoga. I craved connecting with Mother Earth in this way, as I have always felt the most healing when I am at the ocean. I needed to ground myself. I needed to get the energy flowing through my chakras. As a Reiki Master, I had tested my chakras and learned that my sacral chakra was blocked. Big time. No surprise. I set the intention to get the energy flowing there to open it up. I was deliberate in every pose. I held my poses, breathed in the ocean air, and felt the healing energy washing over me. I was present. Savasana was divine. I lay there in the sand, my arms and legs outstretched and connected with the ground. I could literally feel the vibration of the Earth. It was powerful.

Over the course of the next few days, huge welts started appearing all over my body. I found that the bites were from the little bugs that live in the moist sand called no-see-ums. In the South, they call them midges. Over the course of the next few days, more and more bites appeared. Some people get these bites and don't have reactions. But my immune system works overtime. These welts grew large and became painfully unbearable. The pain and itching woke me from my sleep. I wanted to scratch them off, but if I scratched them in the way I wanted to, it would leave my legs and arms with scars.

When I returned home, I looked them up. I wanted to understand, better, what they were and why they do what they do. What I learned was that the female no-see-ums bite human beings to get the proteins they need to lay eggs. *Okay, I get it. It's their life cycle.* As I contemplated this no-see-um life cycle, I thought, *what an injustice that we have females attacking other females for their own benefit.* And then the lightbulb flickered on.

It reminded me of how I felt when I learned about this affair. A woman attacking another woman for her own good or for her own agenda. I have seen women use other women or manipulate them and be on the other side of the fence from them. Instead of lifting them up and straightening their crowns, they tear them down and rejoice in their downfall.

I am around enough people who would love to see me fall— or at least they give the perception of that. I can see envy or jealousy in their eyes when something great happens to me. I don't see the pure joy of knowing that something great is happening to their friend. I don't understand this mindset because I genuinely feel happy for my friends when good things happen to them. And I share in the tears when difficult times arise for them.

I have to twist my way of thinking in order to try to understand this. I guess in a way, people rejoice when something bad happens to others because maybe they don't feel so alone in their misery, or they feel like they are better in some way. Human nature may lend itself to subconscious patterns where people elevate themselves by putting other people down or seeing them fail. The whole concept of women preying on other women for their own benefit is completely disheartening to me. I felt the impact of this when a woman purposely and deliberately did something to hurt me.

But we choose our tribe. We choose our people who are going to stand by us no matter what. Whether we are making the shittiest of decisions or the best of decisions, they are our decisions to make.

So, for those little no-see-um females preying on other women so they have proteins to form eggs and procreate, they make decisions for themselves and their own sustainability and survival. It is a powerful reminder that human nature and animal nature creates this. Their choices, behaviors, and patterns are independent of us. Those little, bitey no-see-ums would have bitten anyone who chose to lie on the sand that morning. They need to procreate to survive.

The women who become mistresses—their choices have everything to do with them. They are either procreating or building their own self esteem up or trying to win a guy to fill some sort of lonely void within themselves. Even if these are fleeting moments, they think that somehow, they can win. They hang their hat on this and hope that the fleeting moments become permanent, and they will no longer be in the shadows of the man's life. They may think the man they are with is the perfect man that they deserve. And I am not blind to the fact that they have been led to believe that there could be something more permanent, whether it was verbally said or it is just a deep wish they are trying to make true. They are not consciously choosing to stab us in the back. They are choosing to believe that somehow, they can reel in this man. They are grasping at anything to believe that even in the stolen moments of untruth, they are less lonely, and someone cares about them…whatever that looks like.

I eventually realized that it truly had nothing to do with me. This was a bitter woman who was just fighting for something she thought she wanted. The name-calling and racist remarks were meant to tear me down in an effort to build herself up in her own eyes. It's amazing how a woman can turn on another woman for the sake of holding on for dear life. This was her attempt to feel adored, better than me, valued, and accepted. This was her attempt to pick herself up off the ground when she realized her imaginary world and her visions of what she wanted for her future were collapsing in front of her. At the time, her racist remarks and name-calling didn't really hit me, but they did plant little seeds of self-doubt that I had to eventually work through again.

Women typically cheat for love. Men typically cheat for sex. And the manipulative interaction between the two to get what they want leaves the mistress wanting more and willing to do more. It's a terrible cycle that will eventually leave someone feeling like they must make a drastic move in order to test the waters and see if they can get what they ultimately want. In my situation, she tested the waters by sending me a series of eight emails, otherwise known as the big reveal. She blew up my world and bet on me walking away.

My initial desire to eviscerate this woman came about from my narrative of the situation being that she did something to me. *Why would a woman do this to another woman?*

She did not do this to me. This had nothing to do with me.

That revelation shifted something inside of me. Nothing conscious. Nothing that I tried to do. Just a shift that has brought me to a place of greater healing.

How do I know I have healed this wound?

Recently, I was heading to an area where she could have easily shown up. The awareness of her popped into my head, and I asked myself what I would say to her if I ran into her. I contemplated. For quite a while. I couldn't think of a single thing. I had no words of anger, no words of revenge. I had no words. Period. In those moments with no words, I realized that she no longer held my power. I straightened my crown and carried on.

Key Takeaways

1. People who don't feel good about themselves try to lift themselves up by tearing others down.
2. The mistress's actions have nothing to do with you and everything to do with her.

CHAPTER 26

CHOOSING MYSELF

THIS ROAD OF TRANSFORMATION IS not for the faint of heart.

When I first embarked on this journey of healing from the affair, I tried to do all of it all at once. Not only did I try to heal myself, but I also thought it was my job to help him heal himself and our relationship. There were three separate entities I was trying to help heal and transform. That meant that there were plenty of times I put my needs and myself on the backburner. I lacked awareness of the consequences of my people pleasing tendencies. I learned that much later. One of the false illusions I had about my role in Nick's life was that I needed to help him heal. I needed to guide him on his spiritual path. But what I eventually learned was that it wasn't my responsibility to heal him or guide him. What he was doing to heal or not heal his wounds was none of my business. What I WAS responsible for, though, was taking care of myself and setting firm boundaries to protect and heal myself. If I could go back and do it over, I would focus on healing JUST ME.

About six years after the big reveal, I found myself stuck in many areas of my life. Sure, I had made progress in a lot of ways. I was processing triggers better. I discontinued the use of antidepressants. I rejoined society, went out with friends, and found joy in my life. I laughed. However, I was still holding on to resentments bigtime. More often than not, when I looked at him, I felt a deep disdain. It had returned. SIX. YEARS. LATER.

We reached a pivotal point where we were both tired of working so hard. Yes, we had some really wonderful times. But we also had some really tumultuous times. And there were several factors that got me to this point, which I was able to uncover piece by piece.

My conditioning up to this point in my life had led me to believe that my feelings were not valued. I knew my feelings were valid. But the mistake I made was that I was constantly seeking validation of my feelings, my opinions, and my choices from people OUTSIDE of myself. In the past, I adjusted my perspective and played the mental game of holding other people's opinions in higher regard than my own. I had always thought that mindset was everything. And I knew that the only thing I could control in any circumstance was MYSELF. To keep everyone comfortable, I always adjusted.

In Brené Brown's book, *Dare to Lead*, she advises her readers to choose discomfort over resentment. What that means is choose the hard discussions that could potentially upset people. Choose the temporary discomfort of engaging and resolving situations. Too often, people pleasers like me avoid those conversations to keep the peace, and we end up feeling resentful of the other person. I laugh as I write this. While Brené advises choosing discomfort over resentment, my tendency was to do the opposite: I chose resentment over discomfort.

I longed for a sense of belonging but chose to try to fit in instead. Fitting in meant that I could conform to any group of people and be whatever they needed me to be in order to be accepted. Sadly, this meant that I didn't get to be my authentic self. I had grown accustomed to saying yes to events, get-togethers, activities, and just about anything, when I really wanted to say," FUCK NO!" I said yes to participating in experiences and being around people that I knew would drain me. I said yes to experiences that were not life affirming for me. I had decades of practice of putting other people first. This was a dream come true for anyone who was self-absorbed or didn't play well with boundaries, which was pretty much everyone I had in my life. Outside of my inner circle, of course. For decades, I had accepted less than what I deserved from acquaintances, friends, family, my primary relationship, my kids. I put all of their feelings, their insecurities, their excuses for being inconsiderate or disrespectful of me above my own needs. I shrank into a tiny little person on the sidelines, waiting for my time on Earth to be done. I chose to ignore the impact that toxic situations were having on me. I muddled through. Eventually, I lost my physical and mental health, my resilience, and my joy. This turned out to be a slow but sure journey to losing myself.

The good news is that I finally reached a point where I had enough of working my ass off just trying to survive. I was tired of the inner and outer conflict, of being misunderstood, and of misunderstanding. I was tired of feeling like I had to fight for my right to FEEL and to use my voice. I was tired of justifying my human experience. I was tired of not feeling good enough to be my authentic self. I was exhausted from participating in events, dinners, and get-togethers with people who completely drained me. My energy was so depleted that I didn't want to get out of bed, and I simply couldn't keep this life-draining pace up. My body and my mind told me that something had to change.

Ultimately, I sat down and made an exhaustive list of all the health ailments that were plaguing me at the time. I lived one of the healthiest lifestyles of most of the people I knew, when it came to diet, exercise, supplements, and sleep. But the state of my physical body did not reflect that. The few biggies—stress management, not feeling like I was enough, and total drainage of life force were staring me in the face. There was no way I could counter as much as my nervous system was taking in, day in and day out, from external and internal messages. I realized that I had done this to myself by choosing everyone else. By not putting myself first. By choosing experiences that had a fulfillment ranking of two out of ten instead of experiences that were eight or nine out of ten. I did this to myself by silencing myself to keep the peace. This was a trauma response.

I had some big decisions to make. For the sake of my life and my emotional and physical health, I had to choose between continuing the same patterns or somehow saving myself.

For my own sake, I chose to save myself.

But where do I start? A wise friend once told me, when I was in the midst of extreme chaos, "Breathe and take care of yourself." (Thanks, John!)

Simple, but powerful words. In times of chaos, when I had no idea what to do next, I had a default action item that I could do. *Breathe and take care of myself.*

It became a mantra of mine whenever I found my nervous system screaming at me. Which was quite often, as I was making the transition from being responsible for everyone around me to being responsible for myself.

The day I started REALLY choosing myself above all else, is the day I really started to heal. Deeply.

Key Takeaways

1. When given the choice to save your relationship or save yourself, SAVE YOURSELF.
2. It is not your job to choose him first or fix him.
3. Learn to say no to toxic or draining people and experiences. Fill yourself up first.
4. Choose to have the difficult conversations and make difficult decisions instead of allowing resentment to build up.
5. Breathe and take care of yourself.

Chapter 27

Using my Voice

For most of my life, I did not freely use my voice when it mattered. I wanted everyone to like me. And if, for some reason, I felt like I had disappointed someone or done someone wrong, I took one of two paths: I either went to the ends of the earth to try to resolve it, or, if I couldn't bear the pain of disappointing someone (which was often), then I completely disconnected from the person and never talked to them again. There was no middle road. There was no talking through things with healthy conversation. Interestingly, I had surrounded myself with people who also did not know how to engage in healthy conflict resolution. Go figure.

Not using my voice applied to simpler things as well. For example, when I was in pharmacy school, I never once raised my hand to ask a question. I didn't want people to think I was dumb, even though I graduated number two in my class. I would ask my (then) boyfriend to raise his hand and ask my questions for me. Throughout my career, I lacked confidence in my abilities and knowledge. I let my (then) husband do all the talking, and I let him take credit for my accomplishments. I was "happy" to take a back seat. I wasn't even aware of the fact that I had a voice I wasn't using, or that I was afraid to be seen or heard.

Two of the five basic needs that we, as humans, have are the need to be seen and the need to be heard. When those two needs are suppressed, it is the most stifling and suffocating feeling. I had lived a lifetime of having unmet needs. And it seemed whenever I asked for my needs to be met, my requests were met with a great deal of resistance, silence, invalidation, and threats of abandonment. My fear of abandonment far outweighed my needs to be seen and heard. So, I silenced myself and found ways to fulfill my own needs or just not have those needs in my awareness. I shifted my perspective.

I had tremendous feelings of insecurity and instability throughout my life that were covered up with a gregarious, optimistic outlook. Those insecurities exploded like a dump truck driving through a nitroglycerin plant after the big reveal.

Surprisingly, as I formed a deep connection with my anger, I started using my voice indiscriminately. The pendulum swung from being silent to the opposite end. I used words and phrases and gestures that I would never have dreamed of delivering to a fellow spiritual being. This betrayal ignited a flame in me that had been flickering for years and for multiple lifetimes. Nick was the lighter fluid. This fire needed to be lit. The house needed to be set on fire and burned to the ground so that I could reach down and collect the pieces of me that I wanted to rebuild and heal. I needed to access the pieces that were meant to be found in the rubble and brought to the forefront to have light shined on them.

I found the authentic, unapologetic use of my voice lying in the rubble. To express my needs, to ask for wants and desires, and to express my thoughts, feelings and emotions. To shine my light on the world with every bit of confidence that I rightfully deserved. To know my value in the world and to know how deeply I have impacted people's lives. I saw that piece sitting down there, and I reached for it and grabbed it. I held onto it like I was holding on for dear life. No one was going to pry that out of my hands.

In fact, when I even remotely felt like people were silencing my voice, which I had not quite developed yet, I fought tooth and nail for my right to speak. I started noticing how I felt in every interaction I had with others when someone shushed me or talked over me or cut me off. I noticed how I felt when someone invalidated what I said, even if unknowingly. I felt a fiery rage re-ignite in me. My voice mattered, damnit.

I became enraged by injustices and atrocities committed against women across the world. I reconnected with a deep feeling of sisterhood and felt the pain and suffering of other women around the world. My depth of compassion for other women who had been wronged or violated in any way grew. And I felt I had to burst through cultural, familial, and societal conditioning if I was going to heal myself in a meaningful way.

The big reveal served as a huge catalyst for me to connect with inner child wounds that I had been living with for generations. The big reveal and the subsequent (beyond frustrating) conversations that ensued needed to happen in order for that fire within me to keep burning bright and to keep fighting for what mattered to me.

During the weeks, months, and years following the big reveal, I ventured out into unchartered territories with my voice. Then retreated. Then ventured out, then retreated. I wanted to be vocal enough, but not vocal enough to risk being rejected and abandoned. It kept me in a state of constant unrest, instability, and discontentment.

I remember the moment when I finally decided that I would not keep drifting back and forth. It was a moment when I had finally had enough and decided that I had to choose my peace of mind. I had to choose my health. I had to choose my authenticity. I had to choose to save my soul. And if Nick left, then he left. I was so tired of the bullshit of having to be someone I wasn't or silencing my true feelings. The bullshit was being delivered *by* me, *to* me. It was the result of five decades of me talking to myself in a less than loving way. I simply couldn't live that way any longer.

The moment arose when we were planning the ceremony for our spiritual union. I was happily looking at flower choices and picking out what color tie he would wear. When I asked his opinion, he responded that the ceremony wasn't something men cared about. And that the specifics were more important to me because women care more about that. I should just pick everything out myself. He showed little enthusiasm for planning any of it. That's when something clicked in me. It was a seemingly small issue, but it was what I needed for me to shift. I told him that I wasn't going to take him anywhere kicking and screaming. Committed couples who care about each other show interest in what the other person is enthusiastic about. If he wanted to do this, then he needed to step up and participate. And if he didn't, then that was fine too. We didn't have to do it. I was fine either way.

I wasn't going to stay silent or play small to keep him. This was different from other times when, out of anger, I told him to go. This time, I was calm and deliberate. This was the moment when I decided I was no longer afraid of him leaving me and the moment I gained great freedom in using my voice unapologetically. Kindly and compassionately, but unapologetically. And with no fear.

Admittedly, I reached this point after years of Nick's encouragement to use my voice. He repeatedly encouraged me to use my voice, especially to stand up to him if he was being unreasonable. He told me not to take shit from him. This was another case of where I was standing in my own way. Pushing against Nick and his expanding worldview. Not trusting. Despite my pushing back, he continued to urge me to use my voice, to not shrink in the face of others, and especially to not shrink because of him. It took me a long time to get to a point where I felt comfortable with my SELF. With the thoughts that were racing in my head. With the woman that I am and the amazing spiritual being that I get to be.

This pivotal moment showed me that from this level of awareness, I could not only survive, but I would eventually find a way to thrive. I could express myself, my concerns, my raw feelings, my insecurities, my doubts. I could talk through them and dissect them. I knew that I would be more than okay with or without him. I no longer worked to mold myself to what I thought he wanted in order to keep him from leaving me. I gave myself the freedom to just be me. And I gave him the freedom to choose what I had to offer or to choose something else. When given the choice, he chose me the way I am. And what it boils down to is that I also chose myself just the way I am. When I chose to accept my voice and the uncomfortable truths of my life, I liberated myself. No one else could have provided this sort of freedom for me. Only me.

What I didn't know for a good part of my life is that I had a voice. And I didn't need anyone's permission to use it. I didn't need anyone's approval. Gaining my voice and approving of myself was by far one of the biggest shift moments that helped me get to where I am today. It helped me heal more completely and feel like my experience was validated. Not only that, but with gaining my voice, I have been able to use it to speak out about injustices such as women's rights, the patriarchy, misogyny, racism, equal rights, and LGBTQIA+ rights. I have more confidence in my views and opinions. I have used my voice to stand up for myself and others in situations where we could have been diminished. I have used my powerful voice to set firm boundaries, to let others know what I will and will not accept, and to choose myself. Not just with Nick. With all of my relationships. Sometimes the person on the receiving end doesn't like what I am saying. But I am not responsible for their reaction. I also know that using my voice doesn't mean I have to verbalize everything all the time. I get to choose when I want to speak and when I don't. I get to choose when it is important to me, given the audience, or when it isn't worth my time and energy. That's called discernment. The difference between before and after I gained my voice is that I know I have a choice of speaking or not speaking, and there is power in both.

Key Takeaways

1. You have a voice.
2. Your voice matters. Find it. Use it. Unapologetically.
3. You are not responsible for how other people react when you use your voice.

CHAPTER 28

THE MIND-BODY CONNECTION

ONE DAY, YEARS AFTER THE big reveal, I noticed that most days my jaw clicked incessantly and got stuck. I couldn't open my mouth without severe pain. Thankfully, I was returning to massage therapy after a long hiatus due to Covid isolations. I wanted my massage therapist to work all the tension out of my head and relax the muscles so I could talk and eat without pain. In the past, she was able to help me with my body pain from the antibiotic poisoning. But this time was a little different. This time, I struggled with pain for months, despite my amazing weekly massages. I had nerve and joint pain inside of my ears. I had nerve pain across my face. I had pain and stiffness radiating all the way up to various points of my skull, behind my ear, on top of my head, and in my temples.

I tried to alleviate this by using bite guards, getting massages, employing trigger point releases, and using heating pads. Nothing helped.

I was really struggling. So, by the time five months passed, I scheduled a doctor's appointment to get it checked out. I had

X-rays. Nothing wrong. I went to a dentist, wondering if I had an infection or an injury that was causing this. Nope.

When everything came back normal, I was confused. And frustrated.

It was about this time my blood sugars were completely out of whack. My hemoglobin A1 C came back at 8.2 despite my trying my best (8.2 is not good). I had headaches and no appetite or energy. I could not get out of bed. I was depressed. *What's with the depression again?* I had somehow allowed myself to get back into a state of funk that I was swimming in a sea of health issues.

I have a book by Louise Hay called *You Can Heal Your Life.* It has been in my nightstand drawer for over two decades. Over the years, I have half-heartedly referred to the back section of the book where it lists physical ailments and what psychological messages they convey. Along with that, for each ailment and psychological implication, there is a healing affirmation that goes with it. I have referred to this over the years and read the affirmations. But I never repeated the affirmations more than once or twice. I guess I just wasn't an affirmations kind of gal—I felt that the affirmations somehow implied that I didn't already believe I was enough and that I didn't feel love and approval for myself. In my eyes, I was convinced that I loved myself already. I didn't need to look into the mirror, look myself in the eyes and talk to myself, telling myself I was good enough. I already knew I was good enough. Or did I?

This time when I picked up the book, I decided to drop my resistance to the affirmations part of the book and look deeper into why I was manifesting physical symptoms of disease. I was bound and determined to get to the bottom of it and figure out how I was going to heal myself physically.

In her book, *Dying to Be Me*, Anita Moorjani describes being diagnosed with terminal cancer. She was given hours to live, during which time she had a near-death experience. Through this experience, she realized the amazing power of unconditional love and joy and what's on the other side. She chose to come back to this world instead of going on to the other world because she decided there was more work for her to do on this earthly plane. She goes on to say that through that experience and gaining unconditional love for herself, she had a spontaneous remission of cancer. I remembered this powerful story and wondered if unconditional love for myself could help me heal physically too.

I decided to take a closer look at the book I was holding in my hands. The one I had owned for twenty years. I took one page at a time. I intentionally dropped all my resistance to what I thought I knew. Because clearly, I didn't have all the answers. I decided to do exactly as Louise suggested throughout her book. I did each and every exercise, and I took my time moving through them. I reflected on what was coming up for me at great length. I made a list of where my lack of self-love was showing up in my life. Some of it was obvious. But there were more subtle things that came up for me too. It became overwhelmingly clear that because of my feelings of not being good enough or not feeling worthy, I was manifesting actual physical and emotional symptoms.

I had some recurrent themes: I didn't feel safe. I didn't feel heard. I didn't feel like I was enough. I didn't approve of myself.

I didn't know how pervasive my feelings of lack and self-doubt were, how much I was holding onto past hurts, and how much I was holding onto anger and resentment. Not only that, but I was holding out on forgiveness. Not only for other people but for myself as well, for basically abandoning myself somewhere along the way.

My jaw problem was what prompted me to open up this book. I didn't have any massages that month because Nick had Covid, and I was quarantined. So, I was stuck at home. I started doing these affirmations and focused on self-care during all this free, alone time that I had. Slowly, day by day, my jaw started to feel better. I got rid of the bite guard. I took care of myself. I kept reading. I meditated. I kept myself open to the fact that maybe there was something to this concept that maybe I thought I was not enough. Even though my mind was telling me I was enough, my body was telling me that I wasn't. I was telling myself in my head that I was safe, and I had a voice. But my heart didn't fully believe and embrace that.

I continued doing the affirmations.

I approve of myself. I am safe. I am enough.

I made a big pile of index cards with affirmations on them. I added to the pile daily, depending on what was coming up for me. What I didn't want to do was read the book, say some affirmations, and then forget what those affirmations were by the end of the week. I bought a little index card pouch and added however many affirmations I needed to on any given day.

I went through ALL of them each day. I read one card, then sat with it. I read the next, sat with it and breathed. Then the next. I literally felt the weight lifting off my body as I read the cards.

Letting those affirmations sink in and saying them over and over helped release the jaw pain. It released the nerve pain that was in my ear and across my face, as well as the gum pain I was having. My abdominal cramps, which had me doubled over in pain, crying, subsided and went away. Only a few weeks after starting the affirmations, the jaw pains and abdominal cramping completely went away.

The mind-body connecting and changing the messaging... this shit actually works.

Along with that book, I signed up for free workshops on inner child healing, feminine and masculine wound healing, as well as a women's reclaiming of power energy workshop. I started reading and learning more about childhood wounds.

I made myself a priority. I crafted a morning ritual so that I could give to myself before I interacted with a single other human being for the day. In the past, I found myself anxious because I saved "me time" for the end of the day after everyone else was taken care of. And often, I ran out of time for myself. So, I got frustrated with anyone who asked me for more. I was exhausted in every single way. And while I was giving to myself in small ways, I really needed heavy-duty doses of self-care to reinvigorate and rejuvenate myself. I learned that if I gave to myself first thing in the morning for a few hours, then I wasn't as frustrated when someone asked me for something. I could deal with it and give more to them because I had put the proverbial oxygen mask on me first.

It took great love of myself to want to keep practicing, keep affirming myself, keep showing up for myself, and keep choosing myself. In doing so, I could heal anything that was happening inside of me.

The big lesson here is that mental health impacts physical health. What happens in the mind happens in the body. Often disease in the body is a result of erroneous thinking and messaging to ourselves. It can be the result of conditioned and negative beliefs that we unknowingly have integrated into our psyche. When we neglect ourselves for the sake of others, we damage ourselves. When we ignore the signs, our bodies are giving us in the form of physical ailments, aches and pains and disease, and continue to push to serve others, we only end up hurting ourselves. Addressing deeper issues that affect your mental health can also help alleviate physical symptoms. Essentially, the most important choice you can make is listening to your body and giving yourself the care you need.

Key Takeaways

1. What happens in the mind happens in the body. Choose your thoughts and perspective wisely.
2. Consider using affirmations to help rewire your mind with positive messages.
3. Put your oxygen mask on first. Whatever this looks like, give to yourself before you give to anyone else.

CHAPTER 29

TRANSFORMATION

M
Y BIG-SHIFT, TRANSFORMATIVE MOMENTS
HAPPENED when I wasn't even fully aware of them.
I only recognized those defining moments when I
looked back on my journey and reflected. Along the way, each
transformative moment felt like an arduous task, asking me
to think about and do hard things. They were seemingly little
steps that added up to a lot of difficult, big tasks. But they were
steps I had to go through to achieve the transformation of
myself. And they were steps we both had to take to transform
our relationship—much like the transformation a caterpillar
undergoes to become a butterfly:

One day, the caterpillar stops eating and hangs upside down.
It spins a cocoon. The caterpillar then proceeds to digest itself
using enzymes that transform it into a liquid. In this state, the
transforming caterpillar is left in a vulnerable place. But without
this step, it can't possibly take the next step. The liquid starts to
differentiate into the various parts of the butterfly, essentially
finding and making the parts it needs to continue the transformation. And once all of the pieces are in place, the hard work of
bursting out of the cocoon begins. In the work of bursting out of
the cocoon, the butterfly gains enough strength to fly.

How symbolic. And how beautiful.

I dealt with a lot of issues when I was lying in that liquid mess inside the cocoon. One of my biggest struggles along the way was that I couldn't believe anything that came out of Nick's mouth. I constantly looked for incongruencies between his words and his actions. If there were none, I kept searching with a magnifying glass. After a few years, enough time had passed with enough consistency that I felt I could start letting my walls down and accept that he was being true. This was a scary step for me. But making the decision to dabble in being vulnerable was a defining moment in my personal healing as well as healing our relationship.

Another blockage for me was that I was holding on to the past version of him, seeing him through the filter of Old Nick. I kept expecting Old Nick to show up and reveal himself underneath the facade of New Nick. I expected New Nick to be perfect. And that expectation didn't allow him to peacefully move through his experience of a perfectly imperfect human being.

For the longest time, I wanted the past to be different than it was, and the longer I held onto that unrealistic expectation, the longer it took for me to accept what was, forgive him, and forgive myself.

Further, as long as I was holding out on forgiveness, I was holding on to the pain. I had clutched the pain close to me so that he wouldn't forget. And so that I wouldn't forget. I thought that if I let it go, then all the transformational work he was doing would stop. And since I didn't want that to stop, I held on. I also thought that managing the pain was a strength. But it was suffocating me.

I finally found the strength within me to let the pain go. Let me clarify a point. At the time, I didn't consciously know WHY

I was holding onto the pain. It was in retrospect that I figured it out and liberated myself from it.

The biggest transformations happen when we choose to surrender. It started with the pain. Then I surrendered my involvement in Nick's spiritual path. I surrendered wanting to be understood. I learned that I could not control his reaction to my words, nor was it my responsibility to do so. I surrendered to the fact that there would be triggers and that there was no timeline. I surrendered to the fact that this would forever be a part of my life.

Surrendering was an important step on my path to emotional freedom and liberation.

But the work I had ahead of me wasn't just about the affair. I had to take a good look at what had shaped me into the woman I was. Not only was I disassembling pieces of our relationship that did or didn't fit, but I was also disassembling pieces of my own sense of being. This might have been the hardest part of the process. It was easy when I could blame Nick for all my problems and tell myself that he was the one who needed to change.

It was time for me to reclaim my power.

Reclaiming my power

The first step to reclaiming my power was to stop blaming Nick for everything and release my expectations that he should be my knight in shining armor. After that, I needed to go deep inside the recesses of what made me. I wanted to go deep because I wanted to excavate anything that was standing in the way of me standing in my true power.

I got silent. I meditated. I asked the Universe to guide me. I asked for peace. I asked the Universe to help me discern between my hypervigilance and my intuition. I wanted to be able to tell the difference and be confident about it.

I dove into the reasons why I had subconsciously chosen men throughout my life who would be unfaithful to me. What, in me, didn't believe that I deserved better? And further, did that part of me that thought I didn't deserve better also prevent me from attracting the things in my life that I wanted? Like the caterpillar inside its cocoon, I had to disassemble parts of me so that I could find the pieces I needed and arrange them in a way that would help me heal and be whole. I had to face some truths in me that I hadn't previously considered. I needed to figure out why people pleasing was so important to me.

I made a list of everything that seemed to be a recurring pattern in my life that manifested as lack instead of abundance. That list included my financial situation, my physical and mental health, the level of joy I was able to feel, my friendships, other relationships, my career and my sense of self-worth.

I discovered that I did not approve of myself. That I did not feel entirely safe in the world. I realized that I wasn't embracing my divine femininity. The things that were causing my lack of fulfillment in life seemed to be lack of love—true, unconditional love of myself and my body. In addition to this, I learned that I had a deep longing for loving, compassionate nurturing. I longed to be loved in the softest, most heart-centered way. I had never had that before. This helped me uncover the fact that I had a lot of internal healing work to do. I have mentioned ancestral, cultural and childhood wounds several times because the work I did in this area was a huge part of my healing and transformation.

I committed to doing whatever I could to uncover the wounds, understand them, and heal them. I looked at my people pleasing tendencies and made a list of how they served me and how they drained me. I searched my past for the first time I could remember people pleasing and why I chose that. I signed up for workshops doing inner child work and harnessing the power and energy of the divine, I researched and read about the divine feminine and masculine within each of us. We, as a couple, participated in a three-month couple's workshop where we took a deep dive into those feminine and masculine wounds and how they present in our current lives and relationships. I did the homework in between sessions and kept the momentum moving forward. It was through this work that I realized I could not trust anyone outside of me to love me if I did not fully love myself first. That I needed to drop people pleasing and focus on pleasing myself. It was up to me to provide that loving, compassionate nurturing for myself. BIG. SHIFT. MOMENT.

I decided to fall in love with myself. I continued the work on myself, dismantling the parts of me that didn't approve of myself. I had made choices throughout my life that did not honor the woman I was or the little girl inside of me that deserved better. After learning that the strong reactions I was having to personal injustices and betrayal were a result of my inner little five-year-old girl not having her needs met, I set out to protect her and honor her at every turn.

Through the couple's workshop, I learned that there are five fundamental needs that every person has:

1. The need for unconditional love.
2. The need to be seen.
3. The need to be heard.
4. The need to be relevant.
5. The need for psychological safety.

I learned new language for what was happening inside of me, which created another transformational moment. I learned how to identify which of the five fundamental needs wasn't being met anytime I was in emotional discomfort, and further, I learned how I could get those needs met.

The process that I am about to describe to you was transformational for me.

Getting my needs met

Identifying unmet needs takes a lot of practice and great awareness. It starts with first recognizing that you are in distress. For me, the distressing feeling could be a pit in my stomach. It could be an energetic shift at the area of my heart, where my chest feels heavy. It could be my heart racing and feeling lightheaded. It could even be the start of a panic attack. It is different for everyone.

Now this is the part that takes intentional effort: recognizing as soon as you can that there is some discomfort, and instead of going down a rabbit hole, choosing something else. Once I am aware that I am having a visceral reaction to a conversation or interaction, then I can step into my thinking brain. Sometimes this is hard. I use my breath to get into my thinking brain and then assess the next step from there. With practice and awareness, the gap between the trigger and response can be shortened. The next thing I do is I ask myself which of my five basic needs are not being met in this moment? I go through the whole list.

Is it my need for unconditional love? Need to be seen? To be heard? To be relevant? Psychological safety?

Sometimes multiple needs are not being met. Sometimes it is just one. Once I identify which needs are not being met, I ask myself a very important question.

How can I provide this need to myself right now?

That is the key. Not expecting someone outside of me to provide this need. Providing the need for myself. This is the part where I get to practice lovingly nurturing myself. But how do I pull this off?

If I can provide the need by dismissing someone's opinion of me, then I do that. If I am really struggling, I sometimes go the route of accessing my inner child and doing the work that way.

Inner child work

The inner child work that I have come to love has been transformational to how I navigate my emotions and soothe myself. In this example, whenever one of my basic needs is not being met, I do my best to think of the earliest memory I have of feeling that way. It is usually me as a little girl. This is where the inner child work comes in. I close my eyes and imagine my five-year-old self in my heart. I imagine how she is feeling, what she looks like, what she needs. It's pure imagination and feeling.

I imagine what I, as adult Sujata, would say to her to soothe her. I am being a mom to myself. This is where I go in and wrap my arms around her and tell her I've got her. Sometimes I might talk shit to her about whoever is upsetting us. Whatever need is being unmet, I meet it. If she doesn't feel heard, I tell her that I hear her and that what she has to say is important. If she doesn't feel relevant, I remind her of her worth. If she doesn't feel safe, I reassure her. I imagine continuing to hold her tightly, with all the love in my heart, until she softens, and until I soften.

I recognized that my five-year-old little girl deserved to be protected, loved, seen, heard, feel relevant, and feel psychologically safe. And my inner child work is important to me. Whenever I stumble, I remind myself that I promised her that I would never abandon her again. That I would walk with her until she truly believed I was there for her, her fiercest protector, her biggest cheerleader. I committed myself to caring for her and nurturing her in a way that she needed. I revisited my past-life regression and brought past-life traumas that my soul had endured to the forefront. I saw how those events informed my subconscious thought patterns and choices in this lifetime. I went back and remembered that I am love. I come from a place of pure white light, a place where unconditional love abounds. I AM that place.

When I first started connecting with my inner child, all I could see was the wounded little girl who just wanted to be loved. When I envisioned her deep within me, I saw a little girl lying in a corner. Timid, afraid, alone. Each time I imagined her, I spoke with her and let her know I would not betray her again. I wrapped my arms around her and told her how amazing she was, and that she was safe. I repeated this over and over. *You are safe. You are safe.* And slowly, over the weeks that followed, I felt her start to believe me. Her eyes started to fill with hope. Slowly but surely, she started to trust the fact that I was her fiercest protector and always would be. There is no one else on the earth that could be that for her.

This is when my inner child and my outer woman merged and became one. This was a powerful moment. When I first felt the merging of the two, I knew I could count on myself no matter what. That I would not abandon myself again. That was when I started to trust myself again. I became my own hero. That is when I reconnected with my intuition, and I felt my connection to the Universe again. I could literally feel the flow of the Universe through me. I felt whole again. I felt wonder. It was so nice to feel that again.

* * *

When I started trusting myself, I dropped my layers of protection and allowed myself to see Nick in his current version of himself. The beautiful, ever-learning, ever-loving, and compassionate version of him. I saw the little boy, his inner child, in him that wanted more for his life and was willing to be better. He was, in fact, better. Just writing this brings tears to my eyes. The veil that had me buried deep under a filter of darkness, foreboding joy, constantly waiting for the other shoe to drop had started to lift.

Again, my biggest moments of transformation happened as I repeatedly surrendered.

I could never have seen this coming a few years ago. While finding out about Nick's affair was certainly a catalyst for starting a fire within me that, at times, raged out of control, our relationship has taken me to the depths of darkness and has also brought me to a brighter light within myself than I could have ever imagined. Learning about the affair was also the catalyst for me to dig deep and heal places in me that never would have been exhumed if it wasn't for him.

After picking up the pieces and assembling them the way I wanted them, the next step was essentially bursting out of the cocoon. I had a new set of expectations and boundaries. They would be tested. There were things I previously tolerated in my life that I would no longer tolerate. There would be pushback. I was different. I was stronger. I had greater clarity. I had a louder and more resolute voice. I was fighting for myself. This was me strengthening my wings and learning to fly. Through this process, I have been able to reveal the most beautiful parts of me. I have developed a deep level of confidence, competence, trust in myself, and respect for myself. I place my health and well-being above all else. I choose me first. I am firmly rooted in knowing that I can handle whatever comes my way. I reclaimed my power by taking responsibility for my own healing, not leaving it in the hands of someone outside of me. Essentially, I fell in love with myself.

It's in looking back at my transformative moments that I can see the poorly wrapped (beautiful) gifts contained within. I have immense gratitude.

Do I lose my way sometimes? Sure. Life happens. New challenges emerge that would test me all over again. I get depressed. But I use the tools I learned over the years to navigate those struggles and return to me. I continue to shed layers of past conditioning and continue to be aware of when I am foreboding joy. *Foreboding joy* is when I am in a moment of joy which is quickly interrupted by the thought of something bad happening. Which, in effect, makes the joyful moment go away. The difference between the not-so-distant past and now is that I don't want to forebode joy. I want to be present, live in gratitude, and enjoy my fleeting moments. I may fall again, but I will always rise.

I do believe Nick and I were meant to find one another in this lifetime to heal old wounds and to help one another along our individual spiritual paths. We were meant to be here in this space and time, to show one another where we had room to grow and expand. We are here to show each other the dark places we each held inside that just needed some light and love to heal. I recall the vision in my past-life regression of the silhouette of a cowboy standing on top of a rock ledge, illuminated by the golden sun, and exuding nothing but divine and deep love. I can feel the love from way back then, during a time when I was content and filled up. I see myself almost blinded by the radiant light. The soul in that cowboy is the soul in Nick. I can finally see it. I can finally feel it. It's so nice to be with him again.

Key Takeaways

1. Transformation is a process that takes awareness and time.
2. Surrender is the biggest, most impactful path to transformation.
3. Reflect on the five basic needs humans have. Find ways to identify when they are not being met. How can you provide them for yourself?
4. You deserve to have your needs met. You are worthy.
5. Consider doing some inner child work to heal your wounds at a deeper, root level. A good counselor can help you.

CHAPTER 30

MY LIFE WILL NEVER BE THE SAME

I HAVE BEEN PONDERING A THOUGHT that I had since the early days after finding out about the affair:

My life will never be the same.

At the time, I was devastated. My life was changing. And I didn't ask for it. I didn't want it. But eventually, I had to adapt.

I had to invite change into this relationship. There was no other choice. Everything had to change. Life-changing events do just that. They change our lives. It is up to us to determine how we want to shape it. We get to toss out old dreams and visions for what the relationship looked like and brainstorm new ones.

As Nick and I moved forward, and I tried to define how I wanted my life to be, I knew for certain that I didn't want my life to be the same. I didn't want the kind of relationship that allowed a betrayal to happen. I didn't want the lack of truly being present or intentional in our relationship. I didn't want the strain of asking for my needs to be met and encounter resistance or defensiveness. I sure as hell didn't want someone who was cheating on me. So, IF I was going to invest the time, energy, and emotions along with the blood, sweat, and tears, then it was not going to be in vain. I was not going to return to something I already had. I wasn't going to accept anything less than I deserved. And I was going to make damn sure that he did the work he needed to do before I invited him back into the depths of my heart.

On the other hand, I felt sad. I used to live a life of wonder and innocence. Rainbows and butterflies. I felt respect and excitement and was in awe of someone. I looked at him with loving eyes. I felt like he was the love of all loves. I felt a deep level of innocence and felt true and utter admiration for another human being. That all changed after the affair. That part was a hard pill to swallow.

After finding out about the affair, I hated all men. I felt like life had finally hardened me for the last time. There was no way I was ever going to let anyone back into the sacred space of my heart and soul. My armor was up, and there were layers and layers of titanium that no one would be able to burst through.

But years later, after a lot of soul searching, I got real with myself and admitted I wanted that innocence back. It lends itself to giving others the benefit of the doubt. When I don't take things personally, I don't have to be on the defense all the time. I don't have to think I am not good enough. In innocence and wonder, I get to connect with my creativity. I get to open my heart and actually experience JOY. And laughter. And I get to take the (what seemed like permanent) scowl off my face and FEEL lightness throughout my soul. I get to re-engage with my children in a happy, light-hearted, and loving way, instead of not feeling good enough. Because let me assure you, when you don't feel like you are enough in your primary relationship, it spills over to not feeling enough in all of your relationships, including motherhood.

There is so much bitterness, anger, hostility, and divisiveness in the world. And going through all these political and racial times during a pandemic where people's rights are being stripped away or threatened, seeing the worst being brought out in many people, I just really wanted to go back to my innocence. That field of rainbows and butterflies that I am sure many people would like to return to.

So how do you get that innocence in a world that is so hell bent on mucking up the water with its toxicity? That was my big question. I didn't actually think I could get there, but I wanted it and I strived for it. Once I had clarity about what I really wanted out of this healing, for me, I feel like the Universe started the flow of energy that would help me get there.

I started to feel the wonder again. The more I allowed for innocence to come back in, the more at home I felt with the Universe. Because unconditional love for myself is the wonder and innocence of everything.

I like feeling like the world is good.

Life will never be the same. When I was saying this before, I was sad and devastated. And here I am years later, thanking the Universe that life will never be the same.

I have evolved. I am more empowered. I have clarity about what I want, what I need, and what I deserve. I have compassion for myself, and I set boundaries that reflect that. I know my place in the world, and I marvel at how the Universe guides me to the next best choice. I choose myself first. I take care of myself before I venture out to serve others. I use my voice. I am strong, resilient, and flexible. While the pendulum had swung to a very aggressive, angry, and protective place, it has now come back to the center where I can also feel compassion for others, I can see how people make choices and mistakes. And I recognize who is truly remorseful and doing the work to be a better version of themselves. I have compassion for those choices, and I allow grace for myself and for others.

I have reconnected with great peace in my heart and soul, and I know how to access it in tumultuous times. There have been more difficulties, and there will be more. That's life. When I am in the midst of turmoil, it just means I am in the middle of that particular journey and that I need to keep putting one foot in front of the other. I know the power of surrendering what is out of my control to the Universe. And I know that I can control one thing and one thing only. That is me. I can control my process. I can control how I take care of myself; I can control my breath; I can control how much love and grace I give myself.

I have also figured out that I can't make everyone happy, nor is it my job to do so. I am aware of my people pleasing tendencies, and I work to make sure I am choosing actions and interactions that are consistent with my core values instead of just doing things to please others. When someone speaks un-truths about me, I can step back and know that I don't have to waste my precious life force getting them to understand me. People believe what they want to believe. People in pain lash out at others. Understanding this, I can lovingly and softly let go of situations that arise that feel like toxicity or attacks. I can stand in my power, choosing what is best for me and knowing that I am not responsible for anyone else's reaction to me. I no longer participate in obligatory activities or gatherings that deplete my energy and life force. My mental and physical health is far more important than making an appearance at something that probably doesn't matter anyway.

I embrace the permission I have given myself to lean into ease. Not everything has to be work, and not everything has to feel painful. Ease is good. Ease is peaceful.

I have released so much baggage, so much of the not enough and not worthy and not loveable. I am enough. I am worthy. And I am loveable. I approve of myself. Because I approve of myself, I seek the approval of others far less. I don't need someone outside of me to tell me I am enough. I just know. I don't need someone to tell me I am loveable. I just know. I don't need someone to tell me I am beautiful. I just know. But when these compliments come in, I graciously accept them. Sometimes I have to work to fully ingest those compliments. But hey, it's an ongoing process.

Everything had to change for us. This change became an opportunity for a new, better life together. Everything from the big reveal to the anger, rage, sadness, hurt and the triggers served as catalysts for tremendous change and transformation. I would have been okay with or without him. But we chose each other, and we forged a way together. And it only worked because we BOTH kept showing up and doing the work.

How's that for some poorly wrapped gifts?

So, it is not just the big negative traumatic things that happen in our lives where we can say with great sadness, "Oh gosh, my life will never be the same again."

It can also be these powerful, amazingly transformative experiences, revelations, and moments of clarity, joy, and empowerment that can also end with an exciting, "My life will never be the same!!"

Key Takeaways

1. Your life will never be the same. That's a good thing. Celebrate that.
2. Get clear on what you really want in your life, and don't settle for anything less. You deserve the world.
3. Look for the poorly wrapped gifts as you move along your healing path. Whether you stayed with him or not, focus on the gifts. They're there. You just have to look.

CHAPTER 31

WHO THIS LOVE
STORY IS ABOUT

T HIS LOVE STORY STARTS OUT with a boy meeting a girl at a soccer field. It is, without a doubt, a love story of two souls who have loved deeply in previous lifetimes reconnecting through the human experiences we have had in this lifetime…to return to each other.

But there is a second, perhaps more significant, love story here too.

It is a love story of me falling in love with myself. It is about the powerful transformation that came from me choosing to save my soul. It is a story about realizing that limitations, wounds, and other people's defense and attack systems have nothing to do with me. It is about me finally realizing my worth and refusing to wrap myself in the insecurities of the people around me. It is about me awakening to my divine beauty and choosing to shine that light everywhere I go, starting with myself. It is about me being kind to myself and giving myself grace for not knowing what I didn't know. It is about me knowing what my soul needs more than anyone outside of me ever could and honoring that. It is about clearing thousands of years of outdated conditioning so that I can uncover the purity that has always been deep inside of me. And when I could love myself this deeply and with such resolve, while I might be shaken to my core with other life events, I would more swiftly rise and remember the truths about myself.

Sure, there could be disagreements. But I would know my truth and stand confidently in it, knowing who I am and how I got to where I am.

This is the greatest love story of all time. Because from self-compassion and self-love, I have my freedom. This is a freedom like no other. It is the kind of freedom that allows my spirit to soar and for me to manifest whatever my heart and soul desire. The light that shines so bright within me can only cast itself into each of my relationships and into everything I touch. This is the kind of light that hopes to help ignite the flames of my fellow human beings who have lost their flicker or are buried underneath layers of conditioning. My friends, there is hope. There is healing. There is not only surviving this sort of betrayal. But you can thrive in a way you may not have ever imagined before.

No one outside of me could ever love me more. This is a love I claim for myself.

I do believe I was meant to find myself in this lifetime to heal old wounds, to propel myself along my spiritual path. I was meant to be here in this space and time, to walk these steps I have taken, to uncover where I had room to grow and expand. I was meant to discover the dark places I have held inside that just needed some light and love to heal. And I accept that there will be more darkness over the course of my life that I will have to work through. I recall the vision in my past-life regression of me being surrounded by a bunch of kids, with the biggest smile on my face, feeling an incredible amount of love and recognizing that I am, in fact, love. Deep, genuine, divine love. I can finally see it. I can finally feel it. It's so nice to be with myself again.

EPILOGUE

RELATIONSHIPS ARE HARD.

I made the choice to stay in this relationship after learning about his affair. It wasn't a popular choice, but it felt right for me. Even so, a part of me was embarrassed for years about my choice. I felt like people judged me as weak or that I didn't have an ounce of respect for myself. In writing this book, I had to come to terms with that. I had to own my choice and stand proud in it. My story is my story.

Working through the affair hasn't been an easy road. Sometimes I think the easier road would have been to walk away. Out of sight, out of mind. There have been many points along the way when I felt like running. But something made me work a little harder on myself, and then on communicating. When there are two people involved, you end up navigating your own triggers as well as the other person's triggers. As of the writing of this book, it has been seven years since the big reveal, and we seem to be in a pretty good place.

One of the risks you run in a relationship, when each of you starts a journey, is that each of you will be ever evolving. Through this experience, you will become a new person. And he will become a new person. Even with the best of intentions, who you each become may or may not be what you want. The new versions of yourselves may not be compatible with one another. Or your dreams may be so big that he doesn't fit them anymore. Or maybe it continues to be a struggle, and you still choose to continue to work on becoming better versions of yourselves.

There are no guarantees. But when you can get to a point where you know that you will be more than okay no matter what life throws at you, then you gain a level of freedom that no one can take from you. You have options. You get to choose your next best step every day.

It is not all rainbows and butterflies. Nick and I still stumble and fall into conversations where we feel like we are at an impasse. There are times when we are both triggered at the same time. That's my least favorite time because both of us are showing up with our walls up. It is beyond annoying and frustrating. It's during those times that I have the urge to run. I have a feeling he feels the same way. Sometimes we just need to hash it out. Getting it out helps us drop our defenses. And I know that once I get a good cry, my walls are down, and we can reconnect. A good night's sleep does wonders for us too. And going out with friends to shift our focus helps tremendously. I love being out with him, seeing the joyful, hilarious side of him. It helps soften me, which is sometimes all I need.

Sometimes I still struggle with triggers. I don't always do a great job at handling them, and Nick falls back on his heels. Sometimes he can't handle me being triggered. But we navigate that. Sometime swimmingly, sometimes not so swimmingly. But even in those moments of me wanting him to help soothe me, I know that ultimately, the power lies within me. I am responsible for reminding myself that I am safe. I am responsible for breathing. I am responsible for calming my mind and my nervous system. I am responsible for remembering my capabilities, strengths, and tools.

These days, triggers don't come nearly as often as they used to. And when they do, I am operating from a much calmer nervous system. I don't feel the impact of them like I used to. I regularly employ my awareness of H.A.L.T. and can make the decision to step away and take care of myself when I have a trigger, rather than wanting to talk about it with Nick. I have found that placing energy in talking about it only makes it grow. I choose to allow it to pass through me if I can. If not, I distract myself by playing Solitaire on my phone, reading a fiction book as an escape, or binge watching something on Netflix. If the trigger is too much for me to handle, then I will bring it up. And when Nick meets it with compassion and understanding, it helps soothe my soul.

We don't always get it right. Sometimes we get it very wrong. But we talk things through. We are quick to get out of any tailspin we might be in and realign ourselves. If it's something we can't get right, right away, then we give it some space. Because let's face it. We can each have good days and not so good days that have nothing to do with one another. We give each other space to settle and breathe and then regroup to talk it through.

When other life stressors emerge, I am doubly conscious of how they can impact the rate of emergence of triggers and the intensity of reaction to them. I make it a point to proactively take care of myself as best as I can. I also keep in my awareness that when other life events get me down, it is easy to go down a rabbit hole of everything that has gone wrong. So, I intentionally keep my focus on doing what's healthy for my mind. I eat well, I sleep, I meditate, I move my body, and I connect with friends. I watch shows and movies that make me laugh or tug at my heartstrings. I want to keep my heart open as much as I can, and those tearjerker movies help me do that.

There are times when I close my heart, and I view it as just being in another season of my life. We go through various seasons individually and as a couple. Navigating them can be challenging at times when my needs don't align with his or his needs don't align with mine. With constant communication and vulnerability, the hope is that we can work through those times with grace. There are still times when we completely miss the communication boat and distance ourselves. This happens far less than it used to, and when we feel the distance, we each want to do what we can to bridge the gap. We both thrive when we are connected. We know that and we crave that.

There are times when I fall all by myself. Even after reclaiming my power, feeling connected with the Universe, being mindful of using my voice, and vowing to choose myself first, I have found myself in situations where I don't necessarily feel all of that. I can tell when I have taken a wrong turn by the way my body feels and how I feel mentally and emotionally. I take the time to honor whatever feelings are coming up for me and I give myself time to go fetal. Once I'm done, I'm done. It's time to get back to heavy-duty self-care and remember who I am.

Marriage is hard. No one said it would be easy. But we are in this together, and we are committed. We are human beings, and we each get annoyed or can fall back on our triggers. But in our awareness and in our common goals, we keep choosing ourselves and one another. Ultimately, we both want peace. We both want comfort. We always strive to return to that.

I decided to write this book years ago. Nick has been supportive from the moment I first mentioned it. At one point recently, I told him I was nervous about writing the book and having people read it and know our experience. He replied with. "How do you think I feel?" We have friends and family who don't know about the experiences we have endured and worked through. And the thought of them reading about it can be nerve-racking. We will, undoubtedly, work through that when the time comes.

Despite how unnerving the thought of this book coming out can be, Nick has been a strong supporter of me writing this book and telling our story. And for that, I am grateful.

Appendix A

Self-care Practices

It is important to have a collection of tools at your fingertips when dealing with a devastating life change. These are some of the self-care practices I connected to and continue to connect with in order to keep myself in an optimal state of mind. These are also practices that I teach and coach my clients on, so they can fully integrate them into their lives and use them in times of crisis, and ongoing for maintaining their health and well-being.

When we take care of ourselves first (put the oxygen mask on ourselves first), then, and only then, are we best equipped to support others or handle difficult life challenges as well as the daily grind.

We are born as pure, bright white light. We are innocent and inquisitive, and we are love. As we navigate life and interact with other human beings, those interactions leave their imprint of conditioning on us. Over the years, as we experience both the good and not so good, we may find ourselves in a position where our light has been dimmed. We have chosen to accept limiting beliefs others have instilled in us. We have chosen to integrate other people's negativity into our own psyche. It is not always a conscious choice. I didn't intentionally choose to have body or feminine shaming issues. It was just the culture.

There comes a point when we realize that our light is on its way to flickering out or has dimmed completely. There comes a point when we look to our younger days and long for the innocence of youth. We may even think that it is impossible to return to that level of innocence, or that it is unreasonable to even want that.

I can say that losing my innocence was one of my deepest pains. I lost my wonder and my positive and hopeful outlook of the world and of people around me. I wanted that back, and I refused to take no for an answer. I wanted to shed the cloud of bitterness and anger that successive life events seemed to bring to me. I wanted to feel joy again.

This chapter outlines some of the ways you can start filling your toolbox and filling your soul.

Contrary to what many people tell themselves, self-care is not a selfish act.

Let me repeat that. Self-care is not a selfish act. Self-care is a necessary part of living, breathing, and thriving in life. Self-care is about every single thing you put into your mind, body, and spirit. It is every thought you have, everything you listen to, everything you eat, everything you touch, everything you smell. It is which relationships you choose to engage in and what you choose to tolerate and not tolerate. It is about being aware of and managing what fills you up and what drains you. It is in the choices you make for yourself. Self-care is a whole lot more than getting a pedicure or a massage. It is a daily practice. Below are some awesome self-care practices that can help you get started to reconnect with your most authentic self.

Affirmations

As I said before, I was never much of an affirmations kind of girl. When I read about affirmations, I felt like they were silly. I already knew this stuff. I already loved myself. I already accepted myself. I already felt safe. Or so I thought. It wasn't until I took a deeper dive into this topic that I realized the very subtle ways that I was actually not loving myself. If you find yourself here, please pick up the book by Louise Hay called *You Can Heal Your Life*. It is an excellent resource for identifying areas in your life that are holding you back and what negative self-talk and limiting beliefs are associated with those particular areas. Take your time reading it. Read a few pages at a time and pause when you get to a suggested activity or exercise. Immerse yourself in the process and give them time to be fully integrated into your psyche. It has taken decades to get to where you are. It will take time to dismantle and heal. Be patient with yourself and give yourself grace.

Breathe

It is amazing how we forget to breathe when we are struggling or under stress. Yet breath is our very life force. Without it, we die. Take the time to learn some breathing practices. After all, the quickest way to change the state of your mind and body is through breath. One of the breathing techniques I teach my clients right off the bat is to inhale to the count of four, hold your breath to the count of five, and exhale to the count of six. Whenever your exhale is longer than your inhale, it calms your nervous system. We don't realize how many times in a day we are not breathing. As soon as you become aware that you are experiencing discomfort or a trigger, stop and breathe. Pause. This will help you get into your thinking brain, which will allow you to access clarity and more creative solutions to whatever you are dealing with.

Make sure you practice this breath when you don't feel like you need it. Wire your brain so that this breath is second nature. It will become your go-to action in crisis and will allow you to move through that crisis with greater ease and grace.

Meditation

I can't speak highly enough about the benefits of meditation. Meditation is a way for you to shed the layers of conditioning that have built up and dimmed your light. It is you connecting with source and feeling the amazing power of it. While prayer is you talking to God or the Universe or to a higher power, meditation is you listening. That is powerful shit right there. This is how you tap into your intuition. This is how you tap into and start to notice the signs the Universe is setting out in front of you, guiding your next step. This is how you connect with the Universe and KNOW that the Universe is always conspiring for your greater good. No, it may not always feel like it, especially when you are in the middle of a shit show. But if it doesn't feel comfortable yet, then just know you are in the middle of the journey. This is not the end. There is a light at the end of the tunnel.

There are different ways to connect with meditation. I teach mantra-based Primordial Sound Meditation, as my preferred method. But I also teach other types of meditation. They are all pathways to access the stillness and silence that is already within you. In times of extreme mental turbulence, sometimes it helps to connect with a guided meditation. A guided meditation allows you to get outside of your own head and just listen to someone talking to you, helping to guide you to stillness and silence. I love this when my mind is going a mile a minute. A guided meditation helps to drown out the sounds of the voices in my head.

I recommend downloading the Insight Timer app and exploring the many guided meditations it offers. Explore several different guides, finding the one that feels good and resonates with you. And if you are so inclined, I highly recommend checking out the guided meditations by Davidji. He is amazing.

If you are interested in learning how to meditate without using a guided app, contact me through my website www.wellnesswithsujata.com for private instruction and coaching.

Sleep

Sleepless nights are to be expected. I had my fair share of them. And when I was suffering from insomnia, I was not my best version of myself. I was more easily triggered. I was angrier. I was not settled. I didn't necessarily make healthy choices for myself. When sleep went out the window, so did self-care. It is virtually impossible to heal from this place of deficit. It is also virtually impossible to have any healthy, productive conversations in this state. More often than not, a good night's sleep when you're in a deficit will shift your mindset, if even just a little.

When your mind is reeling from the aftermath of an affair or from subsequent conversations and distress, getting a good night's sleep can be a challenge. I recommend connecting with meditation or breathing techniques to calm your nervous system and your mind, so you can more easily fall asleep. If that doesn't work, I have had success with turning on an Audible book and having one of the authors read me a story until I fall asleep. The app has a sleep feature which will automatically turn the book off after a specified time.

It also helps to have a sleep routine. Looking at your phone, scrolling through social media, and watching the news can stimulate your brain to the point where you catch your second wind. I have been there. Staring at the clock at two in the morning wondering when I would fall asleep. What helped me was to establish a bedtime routine where I start the wind-down process an hour before I want to fall asleep. I disconnect from my phone, write in my gratitude journal, read a little, and then close my eyes. Once I close my eyes, I either connect with the 4-5-6 breath or do a body scan to relax all the parts of my body.

Getting a good night's sleep is always a good idea. It helps your body repair and helps your mind reset. And being well rested will help you manage your triggers better, as well as navigate life in general.

Visualizations

I used visualizations quite a bit during my healing path. At one point, the weight of the triggers was so difficult that I simply couldn't carry it anymore. I closed my eyes, took some long, deep breaths, and then imagined angels surrounding me. They had these big white sheer fabrics that were stronger than steel but flowed like the wind. I laid each of the heavy weights I was carrying, one by one, on that fabric. As I placed the emotional weights on the fabric, I imagined that weight being lifted off me and onto the fabric. At the end of the visualization, I imagined the angels taking those emotional burdens away effortlessly by flying through the air. Reminding me that they could help carry any amount of weight I was burdened with. If I ever wanted to get one of those weights back, I could do it at any time. But there was no need in the moment, as I felt lighter and lighter.

Close your eyes and breathe. Imagine what it is you want to have, feel, or do. And then imagine you have that. Feel it fully. Let that feeling wash over all the cells of your body. Stay there for five to ten minutes before slowly bringing your awareness back into the room.

Grounding

This is a hugely powerful tool to practice. Just being in nature for fifteen minutes or looking at nature for the same amount of time can lower your cortisol levels. Cortisol is one of those stress hormones that can wreak havoc on your body when you are exposed to it over a long period of time. And anyone dealing with a trauma of betrayal of any sort is bound to be exposed to chronically high levels of cortisol.

Let's face it. When we are depressed, sometimes all we want to do is sit in a chair and do nothing. The slightest bit of effort feels like heavy lifting. This is why I love the practice of grounding. You literally just have to walk outside barefoot, sit down in a chair, and place your bare feet in the grass. And from there, you can just sit and breathe or look around or close your eyes. You can enjoy a cup of coffee. With your bare feet planted in the grass, you will be connecting to the powerful healing energy of the Earth. While you are sitting there, just notice.

Try it today. Set a chair in your yard. Place your bare feet on the ground. Either close your eyes or look around. Take in the sounds of nature, whether it is leaves wrestling in the wind or birds chirping. Sit there for twenty minutes. Enjoy.

Exercise

Exercise is a great way to release endorphins, which are feel-good hormones. When going through something so devastating, we need all the help we can get. Whether it is five minutes or forty-five minutes, aerobic activity, or lifting weights, getting up and moving your body can do your mind a whole lot of good. Another benefit to exercise is this: the body stores trauma in all of its cells. The last thing we want to do is have that energy reside in our bodies long term. It is up to us to keep that energy flowing and continually release those things that are toxic to our bodies. Emotional stress can cause physical damage and inflammation by creating oxidative stress in the body. Get your body moving and keep it moving to help alleviate the consequences of stress and to help your brain feel better.

If you are having difficulty motivating yourself, start by "forcing yourself" to walk for ten minutes. Then go from there. You might find that you want to keep going because it feels good. Or you can move your body in another way. You could put some music on and start by swaying side to side until the mood hits you to dance. Do what feels good for you.

Nutrition

It is no surprise that what we put into our bodies matters. But what do we do when we are stressed or going through something difficult? Many of us comfort eat. We eat because we "deserve" it. We stop cooking because we are too damn tired and dejected to cook, and we end up waiting until we are starving before eating. This leads to making poor food choices and reaching for carbs, sweets, fried foods, ice cream, and other foods that we, again, think we deserve. But this serves as a detriment to our bodies and our minds. Once in a while, sure. Of course! Chips and ice cream were my go-to foods for a while. Ice cream sandwiches became my friends for a long time. But ultimately, you will fare better by making healthy choices. What you put into your body absolutely affects your energy, how you process stress, your quality of sleep, and your ability to navigate tough stuff.

Changing everything all at once is rarely sustainable. Start by introducing whole foods into your diet. You can even buy frozen fruits and vegetables, so you don't have to think about prep work when you don't have the energy to do so. You can find whole foods by walking and shopping the outer perimeter of the grocery store. Look for brightly colored fruits and vegetables. Research what kinds of foods are good for you and stay away from processed and refined foods.

Nutritional supplements can also be of benefit to support your body through your long-term stressful events. I recommend you work with someone who is well-versed in the area of nutritional supplementation or functional medicine, so you have a rhyme and reason for what you are taking. I also suggest that you only purchase highly reputable brands of supplements so you can ensure superior ingredients that have the best chances of being absorbed and used by your body. If you are so inclined, contact me at my website www.wellnesswithsujata.com to inquire how we can work together or determine what solutions and resources might be available to you.

Eliminate toxic people

Look. The last thing you need when you are struggling to get yourself out of bed and function each day is toxic people in your life. You are already depleted. Toxic people will drain you further. They will suck the life completely out of you. If they are toxic to you in good times, think twice about having them in your lives during challenging times. It is a healthy and life-affirming choice to eliminate toxic people from your life. I don't care if they are acquaintances, friends, or even family. I realize that sometimes it is not possible to remove someone from your life completely. In this situation, you can still establish firm, healthy boundaries to help protect yourself from any negative impacts. If there are people in your life who are not life affirming, you have permission to reduce the time you are around them, set healthy boundaries or eliminate them from your circle completely.

Choose more eights and nines and fewer threes and fours

Go ahead and make a list of activities and relationships you regularly spend time in. Make a list of the things you do on a daily basis as well as what you do during your free time, in the evenings, when you head out for a night out. And then looking at that list, rate them on the joy scale of 1-10, with 1 being very low joy or even draining to you, and 10 being the most joyful and fulfilling to you. Once you do that, start to become mindful about the choices that you make. Choose to engage in activities that you rate as 8–9 more often and start to choose fewer 3–4's. Choosing things that bring you joy and reducing the amount of time you spend on activities that don't bring you joy will start to fill you up. Not only that, but when you fill up, you will stay full longer because you won't be drained by the experiences that are 3's and 4's.

Quit tolerating

In life, we are taught to tolerate. From the time we are toddlers, through school, through college and beyond, we are taught that tolerating other people, circumstances, and situations that are less than ideal is the right thing to do. And while it is necessary to tolerate certain situations in order to assimilate into various environments, there can be things that we tolerate in life that serve no purpose for us. Sometimes we tolerate other people's behaviors, which ends up letting them know that it is okay to treat us a certain way. Sometimes we end up tolerating things that suck the life out of us, and we don't know how to get out of these patterns of relationship. It's okay. We have all been conditioned to do this. But we have also been conditioned to do this at the expense of ourselves. At the expense of our own personal mental and physical health and well-being. This is not okay. When it starts to affect our personal well-being, or maybe even beforehand, it is time to stop this pattern.

An exercise I like to do is to make a list of ten things I am still tolerating that don't sit well with me or make me feel less than. And then I go down that list and make a commitment to myself to no longer tolerate those things. That could mean that I step outside for conversations I don't want to engage in, or maybe I don't attend an event where I would be exposed to toxic influences. It could mean that the next time someone says something racist or narrow minded, I speak up. It could also mean that I set new and firm boundaries for what I will and what I will not tolerate.

This can be extremely life affirming, and I did this exercise several times on my healing path. There were certainly red flags that I tolerated during our relationship before the big reveal.

And there were certainly things I would no longer tolerate or accept if we were going to continue in our relationship together.

This all starts with the awareness that you have been tolerating things that don't serve your mental health and well-being, and then making the commitment to do something about it. This is your chance. This is your new beginning. You get to choose what you want in your life and what you don't want. Get clear.

I challenge you to make a list of ten things (or people) you have been tolerating. And then make a commitment to yourself to no longer tolerate them.

Quit making other people's poor behavior okay

This was a big one for me. I had become so accustomed to shifting my perspective in order to make his poor choices and behaviors okay. I had what seemed to be an unending well of compassion for his pain and suffering in life, being abandoned early in life, and the fact that he didn't have effective tools to deal with those things in a healthy way. This combination of my compassion and his dysfunctional upbringing was a recipe for disaster. I finally decided to stop making other people's poor behavior okay for them and allow them to feel whatever consequences arose from their choices. Believe it or not, this is a practice in self-care. You get to be in charge of yourself, and you give the other person the freedom and the responsibility to mend themselves (whether or not they accept the challenge is on them). That is a gift.

As a means of gaining awareness, make a list of when you may have altered yourself or your speech to try to make someone's poor behavior okay for them. The times when you told someone their behavior was okay to ease their mind, when you knew it wasn't okay with you. Reflect on that list and think about if you still have those tendencies. How does it serve you? How does it drain you?

Find moments to connect with joy

When I talk about joy and finding moments to connect with joy, I realize there could be some negative connotations associated with it. I am not promoting what has become known as toxic positivity, where you swallow the tough challenges that are coming up for you and put a fake smile on your face. I am not saying that choosing joy will make the deep hurt disappear. I am a big proponent of feeling your feelings and working through them. What I am saying is that it is important to find moments to connect with joy, so that your mind knows there is a path back to it.

Connecting with joy has been really difficult for me and has been in flux. Over the years, I instinctually learned to forebode joy because if I did feel joy, that would be the time the other shoe would drop. It was a self-protective mechanism I used to prevent myself from being on cloud nine one minute, then crashing when the next terrible thing came along. I was fine with just an even-keeled mood.

But was I really fine? No, not really. I was lacking the spark that made me want to get up in the morning. I went through the motions of the day, only to count the hours until I could sit in front of the TV and binge watch a TV show until I fell asleep again.

My oldest daughter lovingly told me that she wanted me to be happy and not bitter. She wanted me to enjoy my life and see the gifts in front of me. She pointed out that Nick had done amazing work on himself and was a good man. That's when it occurred to me that despite the amazing things going on in my life, I was not able to connect with joy. This foreboding joy had become a part of me. I wanted more. But how?

First of all, awareness is key. The fact that I was consciously aware of my choice to forebode joy and knew that I wanted something more, set the energy in motion. Next up was figuring out how to rewire the default patterns I had established. There are a few practices that I teach my clients that come in handy for achieving this.

Gratitude

Having a gratitude practice is essential. This is not just a mental recollection of my blessings. It is a practice. And a practice entails doing something each day. So, at the end of each day, I started writing in my journal. I made a list of five things that happened that day that I was grateful for. Some days were really easy. Especially the days my children were around. Other days were harder. I had to dig deep to find something I was truly grateful for. That may have included that I had a hot cup of coffee that day. It could have been that I painted my toenails that day. Other times, I found gratitude in big things that happened. Maybe a revelation that pointed me in a new direction or for clarity on my path. And other days it was the fact that I got to spend time with my parents or children.

Having this type of gratitude practice made me search for the blessings in my day and keep my mental energy looking in that direction instead of focusing on things that went wrong. In foreboding joy, a lot of the focus is on what could go wrong. The brain is trained to look for that. With just a little refocusing, it is quite possible to rewire the brain and change your outlook.

I suggest starting by getting a pretty journal that makes you feel good. You could even add bling to it. And maybe get a new set of pens or colored fine point markers to write with. Then, at the end of each day, write down five things that happened that day that you are grateful for.

Doing what you love

The next practice I choose to do is to make a list of things I love to do. It could be having coffee on the deck, painting my toenails, getting a massage, spending time with a loved one, boating, connecting with Nick, playing a game, grounding to the Earth, doing yoga, dance lessons, whatever. I make a list of at least fifty things. And then each day, my goal is to do at least one of those things. Essentially, I start to connect with things that I know have brought me joy in the past. Initially, I had to go into the activity with the intention of connecting to joy and having my brain remember what that feels like. It helped me keep and strengthen the lifeline to who I know I am.

When you first start this practice, you might not necessarily feel the level of joy you were once used to. But you may feel a little smile show up on your face. Or you might feel a little lighter. This is your brain remembering what it feels like to do things you love.

In time, as you continue to process your grief and trauma and do more of the things on your list, you will connect with joy more frequently. And as your brain remembers to look for this, your level of joy will expand as well. Some days I compete with myself and try to see how many of the things on the list I can connect with. I intentionally focus my energy on things that move away from foreboding joy, and slowly I start to feel comfortable with the idea of allowing myself to feel it.

I encourage you to go ahead and make that list of fifty things that you love to do. And then as you work through your grief and trauma, remember to do at least one of the things on the list every single day.

Body practices

I highly recommend massages or other body/energy practices. That could include reiki, acupuncture, sitting in a salt cave, flotation tanks/pools, infrared sauna, etc. Any assortment of these practices can do wonders for releasing stored energy, help heal physical ailments you're experiencing, and help you relax your mind. Whether it is once a month or once a week, make sure you treat yourself to soothing practices.

Yoga

There are multiple books out there about how trauma affects the body and is stored in the body. Often when someone has a trauma anniversary coming up, their body tells them before it even hits their conscious mind that the date is coming up. Yoga is one of those practices that can assist with both mobilizing and releasing stored trauma as well as keeping you in the present moment. The practice of intentional breath combined with intentional movements creates a beautiful opportunity for present-moment awareness as well as release. If you have never tried yoga before, look up a restorative yoga practice online and check it out. Or go to a highly referred yoga class that is old-school yoga. Something that is spiritually based rather than one of the Western, watered-down fitness yoga classes. You want the real deal. *Yoga* means union of mind, body, and spirit. It is not about competition or getting your ass kicked. It is about tuning into your own body and learning to honor yourself and where you are in every given moment. It is about body awareness, mental awareness, emotional awareness, and making conscious, intentional choices that serve you.

It is what you learn on the mat that you take off the mat and into your daily life. You learn to recognize when something feels good, and something doesn't feel good. You develop your relationship with your body, and you start to choose nourishing and life-affirming activities over experiences that are draining. Toxic relationships naturally fall by the wayside because you are so busy filling your life with what you want in your life.

Yoga is far more than doing poses in a hot room. Yoga is a way of life.

One thing you can do today is look up a yoga video online. If you don't have experience with yoga, try a beginner's class. If you are struggling with energy and motivation, find a restorative yoga video or class. There is less effort and more Being, which might be exactly what you need.

Find something you can control, and control the heck out of it

When you are in the depths of despair, and the rug has been swept out from underneath you, and you are the last to know, your world spins out of control. Everything you thought you knew to be true feels like a lie. You have no idea if someone is telling you the truth or feeding you a line of shit. You have no idea what he is doing and if you can trust him. You question almost everything that once seemed real. Things feel completely out of control. You can't control him, and you have difficulty controlling your own thoughts, triggers, and emotions.

We naturally want to control something. So, find something you can control (not someone else). Something that you can control. For me, it was my house. I could control how clean I kept my house. It was important for me to have an organized house so that the clutter around me did not add to the clutter inside my brain. So, I controlled that. Everything else, I let be. I surrendered. I made the conscious choice to let everything else be. Our brains need to feel like we have control over something. It helps us feel safe. So, find something of your own, and do it. Own it. Surrender everything else.

Not only do I teach clients how to use and integrate these self-care practices, I also personally use them on a daily basis. I have found through my work with clients that if I give them a list of things to do to optimize their health, the human temptation is to start doing all of them all at once. This essentially sets them up for failure.

The key to using these tools is to start with one. Learn it. Integrate it into your life so it becomes a habit. Then learn the next tool. Make it a part of your life and make it a habit. Then add the next tool. One by one, as you fully integrate each tool, it becomes a part of your lifestyle. It won't be something that you look to only in times of crisis. They will be tools that become second nature to you. So, whether you are as calm and peaceful as can be, or you are indeed in crisis, or a moment of anxiety, you will be able to connect with these tools or practices, and you will benefit from them.

Another point about self-care and learning new lifestyle tools that I like to remind my clients of is to celebrate the wins. Little wins or big wins—a win is a win. I always start my wellness coaching sessions celebrating any wins from the previous week. It's good to focus on those and take the time to pat yourself on the back, reward yourself, have a dance party, go out to eat, buy yourself something you have been saving for, or just enjoy the stillness of nature.

I have coached many clients through life-changing events. I use mind, body, and spirit practices to guide my clients on their holistic journey to healing. Feel free to check out my website, www.wellnesswithsujata.com for more information on how to work with me.

APPENDIX B

Key points to Remember

If you read nothing else in this book, please read this.

Here are some of the key points and items of self-care I want you to remember or practice. In no particular order. Make it a goal to connect to this list daily and choose one thing each day to keep in mind or to practice.

1. His affair does not define who you are.
2. His affair had absolutely nothing to do with you. It was all about him and his choices.
3. It is okay to try out multiple counselors until you find one that resonates with you, and you have a connection with. It is not your job to make your counselor comfortable. You should feel safe, supported, heard, and seen with whomever you choose.
4. It is absolutely okay to ask for help.
5. No one except for you can make the choice to stay in the relationship or leave the relationship. However, if you are in a relationship that is emotionally or physically abusive, I encourage you to seek help to take steps to safely move out of that relationship.
6. Triggers will come. Imagine your whole body as one big nervous system. It is your job to keep your nervous system as calm as possible. Learning how to regulate your nervous

system will help you navigate triggers and support your mental health during your healing process.

7. Triggers will not last forever.

8. Make decisions from a place of peace and as healthy of a mindset as possible.

9. Trust your intuition. It's your superpower.

10. You are in charge of doing your work, and he is in charge of doing his. Do the work. Use the information you gain in observing whether or not he is doing the work to make healthy choices for yourself.

11. What happens in the mind happens in the body. Choose your thoughts wisely. Do the work to work through your negative thoughts and beliefs, and you can heal your life.

12. Find something in your environment that you can control and control that. When everything else seems out of control, it is important to feel like you can manage something. Your brain likes that. Just make sure you are not trying to control another human being.

13. Betrayal is a trauma. Betrayal is grief. Treat it as such.

14. Find healthy ways to release your anger. Don't let your anger turn you into someone you are not. Don't let the world harden you or make you bitter.

15. You deserve to live a joyful life.

16. Take care of yourself first. Self-care is not selfish. It is absolutely essential to your healing.

17. You are allowed to say no to sex.

18. You are allowed to say no to life-draining people and experiences. You are allowed to choose EASE. Everything doesn't have to be hard. Choose wisely.

19. You have a voice. Use it.

20. You can only love someone outside of you as much as you love yourself. Fall madly in love with yourself first.

21. Hurt people hurt people. Understand that but don't let it be their excuse. Once someone is aware of it, it is their responsibility to heal themselves. And recognize this within yourself as you are hurting. Be aware.

22. If you have a choice between saving yourself and saving your relationship, SAVE YOURSELF

23. Honor your own timeline in your healing journey. There is no set number of days or years after which you are no longer allowed to feel the effects or talk about the effects of the affair. Honor that. And if you have chosen to stay with your partner, make sure that he also honors your process.

24. Don't get stuck in a victim mindset. There is a line between taking the time to honor all of your emotions and getting stuck in the victim mindset. Learn the differences between the two. Go fetal when you need to and keep choosing to rise after each setback.

25. I highly encourage you to take breaks when you become aware that you are sitting in your anger and yelling at the top of your lungs. Pause. Breathe. Step away for an allotted amount of time with the intention of returning to the conversation. Saying the same thing over and over, just louder, does not sink in or help get your needs met any sooner.

26. Remember that triggers have the tendency to get a hold of you more intensely when you are hungry, angry, lonely, or tired. Learn to recognize where you are and meet those needs to minimize the impact of your triggers.

27. Breathe. The quickest way to change the state of your mind and body is with breath. Inhale to the count of four, hold for the count of five, and exhale to the count of six. Fill your

belly up with as much air as possible. Be intentional and deliberate about your breath. Practice for five to ten minutes.

28. You will likely need a lot of validation of your experience as well as soothing of your triggers. The best time to teach your partner how to provide this for you is when you are coming from a place of peace. When you communicate your needs calmly and from a place of vulnerability, partners are much more receptive to learning new things.

29. You are the keeper of your mind and your body. You have the right to say no to sex without guilt. You also have the right to say yes to sex. Do what feels right to you.

30. Remember your WHY. Why is it that you wake up every day? What is your purpose? Your WHY will help get you through your darkest hours. Figure out what it is, write it down, and keep it somewhere accessible to you.

31. If you decide to stay, use the affair as an opportunity to expand your relationship into something healthier and stronger than it was before. A counselor once told me that she had seen the strongest of relationships come out of the wickedest betrayals. Again, if there is abuse, then get out.

32. Intimacy is far more than sex. You deserve to have true intimacy. Get clear on what that means to you and don't settle for less.

33. Remember that this pain is temporary. This is not permanent. Each time you have a trigger, you are not starting at square one. Use the trigger and your response to become aware of what works for you, what hurts you, how you want to respond the next time, what you want to avoid for the time being, what you want in your life, and what you don't want in your life.

34. You will get through this. You will not only survive, but you can develop the tools to thrive.

35. Transformation is hard work. It can take years. Be gentle with yourself on your path and celebrate the successes as they come.

36. Your life will never be the same. Make it spectacular so you can say that with excitement.

37. If you are having difficulty managing your life or have thoughts of suicide or self-harm, please seek the help of a health care professional.

38. You are enough.

39. You are enough.

40. You are enough.

References and Resources

"Coping with Grief: How the Ball and the Box Analogy May Help," Psych Central. https://psychcentral.com/blog/coping-with-grief-ball-and-box-analogy.

"HALT: Pay Attention to These Four Stressors on Your Recovery," Cleveland Clinic, health.clevelandclinic.org/halt-hungry-angry-lonely-tired.

Davidji. Davidji.com/guided meditations.

Hay, Louise. *You Can Heal Your Life*. Hay House, 1984.

Kübler-Ross, Elisabeth. *On Death and Dying: What the Dying Have to Teach Doctors, Nurses, Clergy and Their Own Families*. Scribner, 2014.

Levine, Amir and Rachel Heller. *Attached: The New Science of Adult Attachment and How It Can Help You Find - and Keep – Love*. TarcherPerigee, 2015.

Moorjani, Anita. *Dying to Be Me: My Journey from Cancer, to Near Death, to True Healing*. Hay House 2022.

Insight Timer. https://insighttimer.com/.

Van der Kolk, Bessel. *The Body Keeps the Score*. Penguin, 2015.

About the Author

Sujata Patel is a newly emerging author who writes about working through life's challenges and exposing the gifts contained within. Her passion is in turning her own life adversities into someone else's support and guidance so that they may live more meaningful lives. She loves spending time in nature, meditating, hiking, boating, kayaking, floating on a raft, or lying around on a beach doing nothing. She also loves being silly and sarcastic, laughing with friends until her belly hurts, binge watching shows and sharing quality time with her four adult children, her four great loves. She thrives on connection and on witnessing kindness and compassion amongst fellow human beings. She happily shares her life in Suburban Ohio with her best friend/husband.

URGENT PLEA!
Thank you for reading my book!
I really appreciate all of your feedback and
I love hearing what you have to say.
I need your input to make the next version of this
book and my future books better.

Please take two minutes now to leave a helpful review on
Amazon letting me know what you thought of the book:
poorlywrappedgifts.com/review
Thanks so much!
- Sujata Patel